An Englis
By Jame

CW00448595

Prologue

Major Rupert Stonely came home after a dubious career selling surplus army equipment. Unfortunately, the army didn't know that. He had also expected to inherit his late mother's estate; she, it seemed, had other ideas. Rupert was about to be usurped by a glorified-waiter and he, quite literally, didn't have the balls to do anything about it. Timothy Montague however, did - he just didn't know how to use them.

The Stonely Estate is set in the quiet English countryside, a world away from the problems of post-war Britain. Self-sufficient and off the map, it's traditions and tranquillity was about to be shattered by the reading of the Stonely will. Rupert Stonely, heir-apparent, found himself demoted (for the second time in his life) to little more than a live-in caretaker. His mother, the Duchess, stout in both heritage and proportions, had taken a lover who had worked his charms into her bed and heart. All Major Stonely had to do, was produce a child and reclaim what was rightfully his. Sadly, his gun only fired blanks.

A busty barmaid, a solicitor with an awkward problem, a draconian housekeeper and a trainee customs investigator and amateur bird watcher, all play their part in the unfolding story of An English Custom.

James Henry

Chapter 1: The Reading of the Will

The solicitors' office of Grimsmead & Makepeace was as Major Stonely had expected, dark, dusty and showing some reluctance to enter the 20th century, let alone 1947. Scrolls of yellowed legal papers bound with faded pink ribbon were scattered about in stark contrast to the regimented order of the lofty bookcases, which in turn rose like sentinels supporting the ornate plastered ceiling above. Here and there, you might catch the odd glimpse of the dark oak panels that presumably lined the walls of the inner sanctum of Magnus Makepeace third generation, now the only survivor of the original firm.

'It's here somewhere, I had it only yesterday.' said Makepeace shuffling around in the shadows. He was, it appeared, as old as the office itself. His skeletal form hung with loose pallid skin, and he seemed to glide everywhere as if on well- oiled rollerskates. This together with his peculiar tendency to blend into the background caused much consternation for his clients who spent time trying to attach a voice to a shadow. His old body was also the unforgiving target of sudden spasms which regrettably caused involuntary urination.

Magnus Makepeace wore a nappy.

Eventually, he glided back to his desk, setting down a battered tin box bearing the faint legend STONELY in scratched gold-leaf.

'Now, where did I put the key?' he mumbled to no-one in particular whilst making a turning action with his hand as if one would suddenly appear in his grasp. A silent sigh filled the room from his captive audience.

As Makepeace rummaged around his creaking desk drawers with equally creaking fingers, Major Stonely sitting directly opposite, examined his fellow potential benefactors in the reflection of a large silver cigar box on the solicitors' desk. A gift from his father he recalled. He had found himself in one of those situations akin to sitting amongst strangers on a crowded train; one avoids direct eye contact in case someone attempts to make pleasant but awkward conversation. Not that these were strangers, but then again, they weren't exactly friends either.

To his immediate right, sat Hoghorn - his former nanny and later his mother's housekeeper. He remembered her as having been blessed with the face of a gargoyle and the personality of a harridan; he also at that time, bore the impression she was a witch. She hadn't changed, nor had his childhood impression come to that.

'Master Rupert.' she had said in a low, curt voice when they had met in the outer lobby a few minutes earlier. The Major had almost forgotten he had a first name and hated the dominance her voice still seemed to command. He resisted the temptation to look down to see if he was wearing short trousers and a school blazer.

'Miss Hoghorn.' the Major had replied, inclining his head slightly in her direction safe in the knowledge that she would always be a Miss and never a Mrs. He was, if he were honest, a little surprised that blood still coursed through her veins. She alone, was the sole reason he had been forced to join the army at such a tender age. Hoghorn would certainly never have been in his circle of friends and acquaintances - he much preferred the idea of a circle of firewood with Matthew Hopkins the Witch Finder General looking over his shoulder as he lit the torch.

The Major or just plain Master Rupert as he was then, was just fifteen when he had climbed up to his favourite spot on the parapet of Stonely Hall to have a crafty cigarette. It was from this high vantage point, that he espied Nanny Hoghorn in the old glasshouse, setting about the small secluded garden his mother had encouraged him to keep, with the gardeners scythe... a vision of the Grim Reaper indeed.

The covered garden had been his pride and joy, tended lovingly, weeded with vigour and nurtured with only the best natural fertiliser the stables could provide. It would be unlikely that you could have found a better variety of hallucinogenic plants and hybrids anywhere else in England.

His grandfather, wounded in service, had retired and become an avid traveller and horticulturist, embarking on grand tours around the world and bringing back many magnificent specimens for research and study. The hardier were planted in the grounds of the Hall which were laid out in geographical fashion; Asia, Africa and the Americas in the sun-favoured south, the more central European around the edges, and the moisture-preferring examples bordered the lake and adjoining woodland. The glasshouse was home to the more delicate and exotic specimens.

It was here that young Rupert had discovered the seed cabinet, along with his grandfathers original study notes. The long wooden-framed glass building had fallen into disrepair after his death and had remained largely undisturbed. His mother had, on occasions, dared to grow the odd geranium but rarely ventured more than a few feet inside. She had felt that the few remaining plants that still survived had done so by evolving an ability to turn carnivorous; silly, she knew, but was none-the-less pleased when Rupert started to show a keen interest, it would keep him entertained.

Rupert was certainly enthralled reading his grandfathers notes. He had kept meticulous records on everything he had picked up from exotic climes. His collection of dried seed pods, neatly catalogued, described both the life cycle of the plant and also what happened if you ate them, according to the local natives. Many, were of course completely harmless, whilst others induced varying forms of discomfort, and some, death itself, but Rupert's interest were in those that had, in his grandfathers words, 'Hallucinogenic properties resulting in spiritual imbalance.'

Aware that perhaps the seeds themselves would have had diminished properties due to age and of course, were in limited supply, his best course of action would be to try to cultivate them himself.

His parents, the Duke and Duchess of Stonely, were impressed. Rupert had never really shown an interest in anything for any great length of time but could now often be found in the library studying books on flora and fauna, geography, science and travel. 'Just like my father,' said the Duke after dinner one evening, 'sense of adventure, explorer stuff, do the boy good to get out a bit, learn the ways of the world rather than being mollycoddled here like some softy.'

Rupert was watching through a crack in the door and was disappointed, not in what his father was saying, but rather that the few grains of powder he had slipped into the port decanter earlier was having no effect. He made a mental note to double the dose.

His next experiment would be aimed at Nanny Hoghorn herself, whom he despised as far back as he could remember. His total upbringing had been controlled by her as both his nanny and social tutor in his formative years. Incredibly Victorian with high morals and a dislike for landed gentry in general, stern, foreboding and a force to be reckoned with.

Wednesday afternoon was Hoghorn's half-day. She would be visited by the parish vicar, the Reverend Simms, for tea and spiritual solace in the little grace and favour gatehouse cottage she lived in. This weekly ritual was always preceded with the baking of a herb loaf which she would serve up still warm and freshly buttered. It wasn't difficult for Rupert to slip in some finely diced dried herbs of his own concoction into the mix.

The result far exceeded Rupert's expectations. Within half an hour of them settling down, the peace had been shattered by a loud scream followed by Hoghorn running out across the drive towards the stable block, followed in hot pursuit by the Reverend Simms, totally naked except for his clerical collar and sporting an admirable erection shouting 'Miss Hoghorn, the Lord is within me and I want to put him within you.'

Rupert Stonely nearly fell out of the tree, his only regret was that he alone bore witness to this extraordinary spectacle.

Disappointment soon followed as Hoghorn re-emerged crossing the drive moments later at a more casual pace dragging what looked like a branch of a very battered holly bush in her hand. The Reverend Simms was to depart the parish with some gusto. Rupert made a note to halve the dose.

It was to be a while before he hit upon the ideal recipe. He had planned to market it locally and perhaps make a modest income to supplement his meagre pocket money.

He had begun to supply the village baker with his toned- down herbal mixture for their own version of the loaf that was to prove very popular with the elder residents in the village tea room on a weekday afternoon.

'I don't know what it is, but our toasted herb loaf seems to hit the spot with the ladies - puts a spring in their step.' said the Baker and tea shop owner. He purposely omitted using the word frisky on the presumption that young Rupert wouldn't understand.

'Does Miss Hoghorn ever take tea here?' enquired Rupert as casually as he could.

'Good God no, she would never fit in here socially, not her cup of tea if you know what I mean.' He winked.

Rupert nodded in an understanding fashion that far belied his youth; it would be fatal if she ever made a connection with her herb loaf, the Reverend Simms, the tea shop and him. He sat opposite the tea rooms for a while as the ladies in their fussy hats took afternoon tea. There was a relaxed atmosphere normally unseen at such gatherings of the village matriarchs. One leaned forward and whispered in another's ear, she in turn giggled and ran her hand up and down the salt cellar provocatively, another saw this and slid a sausage roll very slowly in her mouth - the whole table erupted into barely suppressed laughter. The only downside, was that of the baker himself who had long since stopped serving the tables after having his bottom pinched too many times - he stayed resolutely behind the counter.

It had all come to an end of course, Hoghorn saw to that. Somehow she made the connection and he suffered the consequences by ending up spending the best years of his life in the Army in India.

The Major's past recollections were abruptly broken when Makepeace announced with some triumph that he had now indeed found the key to the Stonely box and proceeded to open it.

He reached inside and pulled out a stack of folded papers, and was just about to place them on his desk with some reverence when he was gripped by one of his spasms; it was not dissimilar to that of a puppeteer with hiccups - all the strings yanked together at the same time. The papers scattered over the desk and the floor behind him. 'Oh dear, I do apologise.'

he said and paused for a moment looking in the middle distance while a moist warmth began expanded in his undergarments. 'Sorry about that.' he resumed and ducked down behind his desk, a faint 'bugger' could have been heard if you listened very carefully.

Major Stonely went back to the reflection in the cigar box. Next to Hoghorn sat Denis Henderson, the old gardener's son, boyhood friend, and now presumably the current estate gardener. The Major realised that he indeed owed Henderson a great deal; he was reliable and honest, provided you told him how honest you wanted him to be. He had given Rupert his first cigarette, showed him how to pick locks, taught him the poacher's art and helped him lose his virginity at an early age. The Major had stood in good stead because of him.

As the Major refocused his eyes on the cigar box, he caught Henderson's reflection looking back at him, Denis Henderson did the slightest of smiles and looked away. Oh yes he thought, he may be older now but he still has his wits about him.

Next to Henderson sat Smallpott, Reginald Smallpott, "Two L's two T's" as he always said when he introduced himself to anyone... smarmy little shite.

Reginald Smallpott was a rotund little man with heavily brylcreamed hair and matching waxed moustache. He was also one of those people that you couldn't help but take an immediate dislike to. This haughty man went to great lengths to appear both immaculate and aloof but everyone knew he came from more common stock - airs and graces applied like so much makeup. He just didn't have the bearing or strength of character to carry it off when amongst those of elevation, where he was viewed as little more than a rather irritating front of house Maître d'. But he had developed a skill, a way to endear himself with the elderly and well-to-do with a leaning towards rich widows who loved the attention. Smallpott had done well for himself, he owned a small but seemingly respectable seaside hotel in Worthing - a coastal resort much favoured for convalescence.

It would have been here that he was to become acquainted with Major Stonely's mother and father, The Duke and Duchess of Stonely. Smallpott's eye had settled on the Duchess quite early - it would be a long-term investment with the dividend a fair distance away, but the Dukes health was failing and a bereaved widow was such easy pickings.

The Duchess had been an astute woman and an ardent traditionalist, her marriage to the Duke of Stonely was admittedly one of convenience as it had become increasingly difficult to find partners of equal standing. Marrying beneath ones social status was not just frowned upon but often led to being ostracised from ones peers. The fruit of their collective loins, Rupert was unsurprisingly an only child, an unspoken conjugal obligation.

The Duke wasn't a loving man, he was dutiful when required, which was thankfully rare. To all intents and purposes, they shared a name, an estate and a heritage.

Smallpott's attentions towards the Duchess were at first amusing, bordering on comical but his skill with the female sex soon broke through, sweeping aside doubt and resilience.

The Duke was at first either oblivious of the attention being paid to his wife, or, and more probable, rather enjoying her distraction. At the end of his month of convalescence taking the sea air, the Duchess invited Smallpott up to spend a weekend in the country. The Duke, however, drew the line at 'that trumped up waiter' sleeping under the same roof. A compromise was reached; Smallpott would be accommodated in Riverside Cottage, an estate building that used to be the old gardeners home and now rented out to selective river anglers. Surprisingly, the Duchess thought this a splendid idea and set about adding a more homely touch to the building and getting rid of the fish smell. Smallpott's monthly weekend visits became the highlight of her rather vacant social calendar.

The Duchess could perhaps be best described as a rather robust, sturdy woman of varying proportions with little allure to speak of. The Duke certainly avoided any undue contact as the separate bedrooms would testify - he knew she had 'needs' but he didn't have 'wants' and so she remained unrequited in the sexual and romance arena. Smallpott's timely arrival into her life offered the male companionship she yearned for and if she was happy, then he was too. There was of course the thought that perhaps the attention Smallpott was giving her may stray to something more intimate, even physical perhaps, but he considered this a reasonable trade-off and as long as it remained unspoken, unseen and not under his roof, he would simply turn the proverbial blind eye.

The Major's train of thought was once again broken by Makepeace.

'Now let me see.' said Makepeace, 'Mr. Reginald Smallpott, present, Miss Chastity Hoghorn, present,' The Major smiled inwardly, Chastity - that was apt.

'Denis Henderson,' continued Makepeace, 'and Your Grace, the Duke of Stonely.'

'Just Major will be fine.'

The Major had been a Duke since the death of his father but had never used the title whilst in the army; it made him far too noticeable and besides, being addressed as Major, Your Grace the Duke of Stonely by a superior officer always felt uncomfortable for both parties.

'I'll skip the normal formalities and get straight to the crux of the matter shall I?' said Makepeace, almost daring them to disagree but knowing full well that they were only interested in what they were going to leave his office with, besides he now found himself in some personal discomfort.

The temptation was there of course, many a time Magnus Makepeace had managed to string out a simple reading for a couple of hours, explaining legal terms in unnecessary depth. Today though, he had more pressing things on his mind, particularly in the gentleman's waterproof undergarment department that was starting to weigh heavy and leak, despite what the mail order advertisement had claimed.

'As you are all aware, the Hall, estate, finance, goods and chattels herewith known as "The Estate", passed directly to the Duchess of Stonely on the unfortunate demise of His Grace, the Duke some five years past.' said Makepeace reading with his eyes and summarising with his mouth.

'Her Grace, the Duchess,' he continued 'had always held the desire that the Stonely family line would have been taken up beyond that of her only son Rupert, who she had hoped would bless her with a Grandchild.' - there was a slight pause in case an heir apparent were to materialise in front of one and all - nothing happened.

'But alas it was not to be, however…' he continued stretching the word longer than strictly necessary, 'The estate will be held in trust and administered by this office for a period of five years in order to allow time for the possible production of such an heir….' paused Makepeace looking at the Major and quickly away. The thought of the Major in 'production' was not a welcome one.

There was an uncomfortable silence which normally he would have enjoyed immensely, but he had felt one of the elasticated straps of his support slowly losing its grip.

'In the meantime,' he continued breaking the tension, 'Your Grace,' he paused momentarily, 'Major Stonely I mean,' giving the Major his preferred title but seemingly not his inheritance, 'will have full use of the Estate and a limited allowance during the forthcoming five year period. This is to include the retention of the current staff who will receive a reasonable reward whatever the, outcome. However, should they choose to leave the employ of the Estate within the aforementioned period, then only a years wage will be paid in recompense of services rendered.'

'And if no such heir is provided?' asked the Major realising Makepeace had dropped a bombshell that had yet to fully explode.

'And if,' took up Makepeace, 'you should fail to produce an heir or prove the presence of an existing one, then the total estate, chattels etc, will pass directly and unconditionally to Mr. Smallpott. You yourself Major will be permitted to live rent-free in one of the gatehouse cottages and receive a small annuity to supplement your military pension.'

The Major sat stunned in disbelief forcing himself to stare directly ahead and control his breathing. He became aware of the pain of his own finger nails digging into the palms of his hands. To top it all, he swore he could actually hear Smallpott smiling. Smallpott, on the other hand, was elated and struggled like the Major to keep his composure. He had expected some financial reward for his endeavours, a few thousand perhaps or at best the freehold to Riverside Cottage. He had also gone out of his way on several occasions with the Duchess, to impress upon her just how much he admired a particular painting, claiming he knew little of art and merely admired the landscape this Constable chap had painted. Now it looked as if he had a chance to get everything. It was all beyond his wildest dreams, an admirable throne for a peacock king.

'Well I won't keep you any longer, I'm sure you all have important things to do.' said Makepeace snapping his audience out of their collective bewilderment. 'My clerk will forward you each a copy of the will.' he finished, almost rising from his desk but stopping short as a cold sodden undergarment slid down the inside of his trouser leg.

For a moment no one moved, the reading of the will had come to an abrupt end, almost as if Makepeace had turned the final corner and galloped at full tilt towards the finishing line, most out of character, almost rude.

Outside the solicitors' office, the beneficiaries, if that term were practical in anyway, stood momentarily. An awkward silence ensued.

'I imagine you'll be going straight to the Hall then Your Grace' asked Smallpott trying to break the ice.

'No, things to do.' replied the Major looking straight over the little mans head, adding a layer of frost to the ice. With that he turned and strode purposely away - he didn't quite know where he was going but as long as he parted company from Smallpott and Hoghorn, he was happy.

'Get the car Henderson,' said Hoghorn without looking at him, 'we're going back to the village.' It was a statement that brooked no argument. Henderson hated her; she had a way of belittling people irrespective of their station in life.

'Ma'am.' was the politest he could come up with at short notice. That left just her and Smallpott alone on the pavement.

The Major watched their reflection in a shop window he was passing further down the street. He noted that she moved a little closer to Smallpott, which was odd; she usually maintained a well-defined personal barrier.

After wandering around for a couple of hours mulling over the results of the reading, he found the hotel he'd been staying at. On his initial arrival back in England, he had resided at his London Club of which he automatically became a member of at birth, such was the privilege of his fathers lineage. He had chosen not to move directly into the Hall but instead find his feet and become a little more accustomed to civilian life. Now however, he had found himself in the town of Stoneleigh, a short distance from the village for the official reading of the will. Back in his room, he sat down at the desk and opened the letter from the solicitor's office that had been waiting at the reception desk in the lobby - his copy of the will. Interestingly, there was another letter inside. In contrast to the neatly typed will, this letter was hand written by Magnus Makepeace himself.

Your Grace, Duke of Stonely.

Please forgive the informality of this correspondence. I'm sure you will appreciate the directness of my approach. Your late mother's last will and testament, although unusual in its content, remains legally binding. It was drawn up in my presence and witnessed by my staff and your mothers doctor. There were no opportunities for external influences and she was adjudged as being of sound mind.

You will note that a monthly allowance of £300 will be paid to yourself for personal use during this period. The entire Hall's running costs such as food, staff and general services are to be paid directly from the estate purse through my office.

If, by whatever means, an heir to the estate should materialise, the final discussion of acceptance will rely on suitable evidence put before me or my successor.

I have had the honour of dealing with the Stonely family and estate for some considerable time and my loyalty in such does not waiver, however despite this I am duty bound to see through your late mothers wishes no matter how disagreeable the probable outcome.

I remain your humble servant,
Magnus Makepeace

'Well that's clear', thought the Major - he was trussed up and buggered like some festive turkey. It was incredulous that Smallpott should even have figured in his mothers will, let alone benefit. He had it seemed underestimated Smallpott's talents and his mother's late romantic inclination and sexual frustration.

Somehow, he had to do the impossible and prove that Smallpott had engineered the whole thing.

What he needed was Major Waller-Boyce, a specialist in investigating people, a man who had an uncanny knack of separating the wheat from the chaff and finding gold. Unfortunately, he was also someone he could never ask, especially as he himself had deceived and corrupted the most formidable organisation in the world, the British Army from within its very ranks with his black market operations and all right under Waller-Boyces's nose. It would be tantamount to putting his own head in the lions mouth. A man who could have been his saviour could also be his hang-man.

With that thought, he ordered a bottle of malt whisky and drafted a letter to an ex-military friend and member of his London club who owed him a favour. It was in the vague hope a little background digging might turn up a clue or a weakness he could exploit. He knew it would be a near impossible task, he had himself spent a great deal of time covering his own tracks and Smallpott was no fool.

Presently, there was a knock at the door.

'Your refreshment, Sir.' called a voice.

'The Major opened the door and allowed the hall waiter to place the tray and small ice bucket on the table.

'A Mr. Henderson left this for you, Sir.' and presented him with a padded envelope.

'Thank you.' replied the Major. The waiter left without waiting for the usual tip - he knew the Major was of the gentry class and tipping every time was seen as vulgar. Cautiously, the Major opened the envelope. It contained keys - car keys.

'Ah, the Bentley.' he still had at least one ally in this civilian battlefield.

Chapter 2: GHQ India

For Major Waller-Boyce, the army had shaped his life and made him the man he was - an upright, authoritative figure with handsome facial-features, sporting a pencil-thin Clark Gable moustache. Unlike many officers his age who leaned towards the more spherical side, he was still physically fit with a broad chest, narrow waist and a lightly-tanned complexion. He personified the perfect military officer, a man in command of men. However, for the past year, he'd been in command of a desk; it was a mighty fine desk, but a desk nonetheless.

The British Raj was drawing to its faithful close and his office at GHQ India had been no exception, it was a situation he found himself reluctantly drawn into. Having spent the greater part of his military career in the intelligence division, he felt his talents were sorely misdirected as he became absorbed into the administration process for the slow but inevitable hand-over of India - to India.

He was now in effect little more than a paper-wallah amongst many others. He hankered for just one more investigation that would take him away from the tedium, at least temporarily, and stimulate his mind again before it too was packed up in a box labelled 'No longer required.' He'd been contemplating retirement and returning home to England. Not that he had a home to return to.

The Waller-Boyce's had a small estate in the countryside, but a heavy investment in 'Spanish Amalgamated Lemons' had turned sour and his parents died penniless, leaving young Winston Waller-Boyce the last of the line and homeless. Joining the Army at his earliest opportunity gave him the reliability of three meals a day and a roof over his head most of the time. The Army was his family and his home, mentally and physically. Truth be known, he dreaded the inevitability of having to look after himself.

Prior to his current dilemma, his duty had been to investigate the misappropriation of funds and equipment from within. He was very good at it, his personable demeanour easily disarmed the most defensive of suspects and working alone gave him the flexibility to travel unhindered and relatively unnoticed, easily slotting into place wherever he was as if he had always been there. The simple ability to disguise his physical appearance with just the use of ill fitting uniforms and a change of posture enabled him to blend in easily with the lower ranks when required.

It hadn't always been necessary. Sometimes just being there was enough. One chap on seeing the Major approaching with a file of paperwork under his arm, immediately confessed to embezzling NAAFI funds to support his horse racing addiction. Others however, became exposed because of careless clerical errors. He had, quite by chance, discovered a Commanding Officer who had attended a cricket match at Lords whilst still signing requisition forms in West Bengal. That officer 'retired' the next day on advice from above whilst his acting double, an adjutant, remained in place as he was doing such a good job.

Real investigations however, were now few and far between, and during the ever-expanding lulls he found himself desk-bound with administrative work making his fellow officers very uncomfortable indeed. It had come as a pleasant surprise when the Brigadier sent for him.

'Bit of a mess,' he said as the Major entered the room, Waller-Boyce looked down at his perfect uniform.

'Not you Major, some damned supply depot in some godforsaken part of this country seems to have gone tits up. Want you to pop over and take command, investigate, sort out the problem, your usual sort of thing, take as long as you need, normal rules, leave tomorrow.'

'Yes Sir.' replied the Major, suppressing a smile.

The 'normal rules' meant he had carte blanche to do anything at whatever cost - it was better than setting fire to his desk, as he had planned to accidentally do later that afternoon.

'My nephew, Captain Bartholomew, is already there, he'll close down the camp when you've finished. He's new, try not to break him.' added the Brigadier dismissing him.

Three days later in Northern India.

'I'm sorry, did you just say a lorry Captain?' asked Major Waller-Boyce in a slightly astonished voice, implying his hearing was failing him.

'Yes Sir, looked everywhere for it,' answered Captain Bartholomew feeling somewhat responsible, which of course he was.

'Lorries aren't particularly noted for their abilities to wander off are they?'

The Captain wasn't sure if this was a question or a statement and fought for something to say that would fall in the middle ground. 'Not as a general rule, no Sir.' seemed suitable.

'Carry on with the inventory, let me know the full results when you have them Captain.' finished the Major who had been rifling through the last Commanding Officers desk, a man notable by his absence.

Major Waller-Boyce was being a tad harsh on the freshly minted Captain but this was one of his styles. He would slowly soften up and give the appearance of 'warming' to him. It was good to keep in practice.

Captain Bartholomew had been freshly dispatched from Sandhurst with a mind full of military tradition and a brain full of fluff. He was a painfully thin, pale young man who seemed to lack a discernable chin, a sure sign of upper-class in-breeding. Now, dressed in desert fatigues, he was almost an object of ridicule. He gave the impression that if he turned too quickly his uniform would remain facing the other way. He was keen of course and had read all the right books, but it's experience not text, that makes a good officer. Confidence comes a close second and it looked like he'd forgotten to pack both. Captain Bartholomew knew how to wear a dress uniform and even how to iron it; they taught him to fire a gun if absolutely necessary and then gave him a sword, which on parade made him drift off to one side - Bartholomew was not a natural. He was officer material because his father was in the right bed at the right time. Now, three weeks after passing out, he found himself in charge of a supply depot in Pongee that seemed to be rather short of supplies, to wit, one lorry – mobile catering – for the use of.

He had arrived just a week earlier as Acting Second-in-command to prepare everything for the CO when he arrived. His tasks were to establish an inventory of the camp, maintain discipline amongst the men and make sure there was tea. So far he had managed the tea problem successfully. The new CO, Major Waller-Boyce had arrived that morning, and it wasn't going well.

Pongee was at the back of beyond. If Bombay was the gateway to India then Pongee was the back-door where the rubbish bins were kept. Major Waller-Boyce had driven to Pongee, there had been no alternative. The single railway line that reached into this desolate part of Northern India had long since fallen out of use and so a rutted dirt track was his only option. It occasionally nudged up against the old track where some small communities still remained in what had once presumably been way-stations along the route, in a similar way towns clustered around rivers, only this steel river no longer flowed.

On arrival, Waller-Boyce had expected little more than a simple army compound with a few huts and some sort of storage building, and what he saw surprised him. Pongee was a small bustling village with a central bazaar and clusters of ramshackle buildings on three sides, the compound making the fourth on the southern approach.

The Army camp had been built about 60 years previously on the site of an abandoned outpost of the British East India Company. Its isolated position had become the ideal solution for the storage of surplus military equipment. It was also where the old railway track eventually terminated. It was literally and symbolically, the end of the line.

In its heyday, if such existed, it had the facility to store anything and everything, but those times had long passed and now it was a dumping-ground for outdated equipment, itchy army blankets, collapsible field kitchens, the 'wrong type' of ammunition and tents so old, the very canvas would crack and snap if unfolded. If it was in the way, it was sent to Pongee for safe-keeping. Waller-Boyce was soon to learn that this applied to everything.

The Major knew immediately that it was ripe for black-market dealings. From the contents of the absent commanders' desk he started to get a picture that it wasn't just out of date equipment stored here, it was a wasteland for soldiers too. A convenient repository for those difficult to place - men that were an embarrassment to the army, the slow of mind, the faint of heart, the directionally challenged and goat shaggers. The camp was a loose end that would eventually need tiding up and tucking away and presumably he was here to find someone to blame and bring them out into the open so it could be covered up. Later that first evening, the Captain returned. Unsurprisingly, the news was not good.

'I think it may have been more than just one lorry missing sir.'

'At least three.' replied the Major not looking up from his desk.

'Oh' said the Captain, 'May I ask how you knew it was three Sir?' instantly regretting it.

'There are five in the photograph behind me Captain.'

'Ah.' was the best Bartholomew could muster, looking at the large picture above the CO's head, something he had failed to notice before.

'Fortunately for us, someone took a picture, rather ironic wouldn't you say Captain?'

'Yes, somewhat Sir' he replied not really understanding the meaning of the word.

'Notice the position of the water tower used for the locomotive train?'

The Captain looked closely for a while until the penny dropped. 'Ah, the tower, it's inside the compound there but it's outside now. Seems like a lot of hard work just to move it a few feet?' he answered rather pleased with himself.

'Rather pointless I would say.' continued the Major, 'In fact, I think you'll find it's the compound that's moved, not the tower.' The Major paused to allow the idea to sink into the Captain's head. He looked up hoping Bartholomew's mouth wasn't gaping open - predictably, it was.

'The perimeter fences obviously, not the buildings themselves.' added Waller-Boyce for extra clarity.

'Oh, gosh yes, I see now.' he said finally.

'It appears that the compound has mysteriously shrunk. I think tomorrow we had better do a spot of measuring.' The "we" in this case only applied to the Captain.

As Bartholomew took his leave, the Major wondered if the Brigadier had sent his nephew here to slowly close down the camp as he had said or to be some sort of understudy pending his not too distant retirement. He hoped the former was true; he'd have to cancel his retirement altogether otherwise.

The next morning, the Major stepped through to the CO's office from the attached quarters behind, to see the Captain diligently pacing the parade ground, clipboard in hand.

The compound itself was the simple but functional square, a design popular since the Romans. The men's barrack blocks ran along the north edge abutting the village market place, separated by a tall fence and the backs of the trader's huts. The officer's quarters and CO's office were directly opposite on the southern boundary across the open central parade ground. The western edge was home to three large tin-covered storage sheds. The eastern boundary, in contrast, was devoid of structures other than a small wooden hut that served as the guard house next to the un-gated entrance on the south-eastern corner - the one the Major had driven through unchallenged the day before.

A tall wire-mesh fence topped with barbed wire enclosed the whole area. The Major assumed the tall water tower had doubled as the watch tower when it originally stood within the bounds. Not that one was really necessary as any heavy movement in the distance created a cloud of dust in this arid north Indian landscape, visible for miles. It had been unofficially repurposed to supply water to the growing Indian community that now vastly outnumbered the military.

Camp WDP/244-India, as it was officially known, wasn't built to stop people getting in but rather to stop equipment disappearing out, hence its isolation and anonymity. Both of which now failed dismally.

The Major stepped out into the harsh morning sunlight and waited for Captain Bartholomew to approach.

'Morning Sir.' said Bartholomew snapping to attention with a smart salute.

'Captain,' replied the Major not bothering to return it, 'and what have we discovered this morning?'

'Well Sir, I calculated a scale from the photograph on the wall and then measured both the north and west boundaries which would give the square footage of the total area. Assuming the compound was still a square which it is, and using this calculation against the . . .'

'Just the result will do.' interrupted the Major.

'About a third missing Sir'

'Thank you Captain, shall we go for a walk?' It wasn't really a question.

They strode around the outside perimeter of the camp until they were opposite the barrack blocks on the north side. Behind them stood the back of the ramshackle-looking huts that made up the bazaar on one side of the village square.

'Do you know how many barrack blocks there should be Captain?' enquired the Major.

'Just three Sir. I understand two are used for storage and the other, block C, for the men.' he replied.

'I see. I wondered why the worn path between each of these three blocks continues to the boundary fence and then carries on beyond. I'm mindful to think that perhaps the barracks themselves were shall we say, a little longer than they are today Captain.'

Bartholomew instinctively looked down at the ground and then behind him. The faint and shallow compacted path was still just visible. It continued between the corrugated covered trader's huts and into the bazaar. Bartholomew looked up at Major Waller-Boyce who just smiled at him knowingly. The Captain then moved along behind the huts, pacing the width of each as he went, the Major followed.

'You don't think that . . .' The Captain's voice tailed off in disbelief.

'I do indeed Captain, very much so.'

The Major bent down and with a little effort bent up one corner of the battered corrugate sheet enough to reveal a stout wooden frame underneath.

'Well I'll be . . . they stole our huts.' said the somewhat nonplussed Captain.

'A third off of the end of each at least and I don't think they stole them, I'm rather inclined to think they were sold.'

'But that would mean someone in the camp . . .'

'Precisely, my dear Watson.' answered the Major.

'Bartholomew Sir.' corrected the Captain.

'Yes Captain Bartholomew.'

Waller-Boyce had revelled in watching him 'discover' what he had seen as the bleeding obvious. He surmised to the Captain that the buildings and possibly other items, had been sold to the growing local population and to disguise what would have been an obvious gap they simply moved the fence. The buildings were then stripped of their external planking and then covered up in the more traditional corrugated tin sheets disguising their true roots.

Bartholomew remained open-mouthed. The Major could see that this young, green officer could, on occasions, put two and two together all by himself; just sometimes he seemed to subtract one for good measure.

The pair then went into the bazaar itself. It was a typical Indian market place. Dried fruit, vegetables, fabrics, spices, bicycles, fuel cans, tents, army blankets, webbing, empty ammo boxes, rubber piping, packing cases, saucepans, tin plates, pumps, brassware and small hand-carved wooden animals. It was the last item that took the Major's interest. He purchased a carved wooden elephant on a brass base with copper tusks.

The Captain, ever keen, had tried to argue with one stall holder that the items on sale belonged to the British Army and that he would turn a blind eye if he returned them straight away. This was the time when of course the native Indians forgot how to speak English.

Later back in the CO's office the Captain was making the Major a cup of tea.

'But surely Sir, to lose that amount of equipment would have been impossible not to notice….. unless,' he laughed, 'everyone was involved?'

'You're getting better at this.' answered the Major.

He almost had to order the Captain to sit down and relax. Major Waller-Boyce then proceeded to tell Captain Bartholomew about his real position in the army, his time in the intelligence department and a handful of his successes, not to impress him but to open his eyes to the wider scope of pilfering for profit. Bartholomew sat aghast at these revelations, his picture of the armed forces soiled, its dirty laundry hung out to dry.

'I tried to get myself attached to the Intelligence Department when I left Sandhurst' revealed the Captain, 'but I failed the entrance test.'

'How did you manage that?' asked the Major with interest.

'I couldn't find the exam building.'

The next morning in the CO's office, Major Waller-Boyce was sat at his desk sorting paperwork. The clerical side of the job was one he didn't particularly relish but it often revealed things of interest - in this case it wasn't what was there, but what wasn't. Captain Bartholomew sat at his smaller desk to one side of the Major's.

'Have you found out yet how many soldiers are meant to be billeted here Captain?' enquired the Major.

'Thirty Sir,'

'And how many have you actually seen?'

'14 at roll-call, the other 16 are apparently on leave Sir, I'm a little surprised that you hadn't taken more interest in the men, if I may be so bold Sir.' said the Captain who realised he was being condescending to a superior officer.

The Major smiled at Bartholomew's embarrassment.

'We have the advantage of being able to look around unhindered without people moving things about behind our backs.' He answered and added, 'What do we know about the CO?'

The Captain was a little more at ease now, he'd found that the Major's relaxed attitude had started to make him feel more comfortable, perhaps he was warming to him.

'A Second Lieutenant Withers Sir. Acting. Been in charge for some five years. I spoke to some of the men when I arrived, no-one seems to know where he was, in fact, some didn't even know who he was.'

'Withers, bugger I should have known that.' expressed the Major with some passion. He steepled his fingers together, almost in prayer. 'I had him sent away to keep him out of trouble.'

'A problem was he Sir?' asked Bartholomew.

'Oh yes, he was a procurement specialist, he could get hold of almost anything. Trouble is, it wasn't always through the right channels - black-market dealings and so forth. Hard to prove of course, always covered his tracks well, it was me that recommended he was sent somewhere distant and preferably at the end of the supply chain rather than along it.'

'Do you think that he's behind what's been going on Sir?'

'Oh yes undoubtedly. If he's had a free hand here he would have set up some sort of empire, this place is ideal. I have no doubt whatsoever that this has his name stamped all over it. When was the last inspection Captain?'

'An audit inspection five years ago - a Major Stonely.'

'Rubber Balls Stonely.' said Waller-Boyce with a slight smile.

'You know him Sir?'

'Of him, yes, I never met him although his name crossed my field of interest a couple of times. Rose through the ranks quickly but managed to get himself demoted to Major after some scandal with his Commanding Officers wife I believe. Spent the rest of his career as a glorified supplies clerk pushed from pillar to post doing audits. He was in the ideal position to turn things to his personal advantage but there's not a mark against him - books always impeccable. That's why I watched his audit reports.'

'Too perfect Sir?'

'Almost. The odd case of whisky would go adrift and end up in the officer's mess for some regimental dinner - normal practice, nothing I'd take an interest in, he was trusted in that respect. In fact, I used his services indirectly to check up on other people, even I trusted him.'

'You said 'was' Sir?'

'Indeed. Last I heard he'd retired back to England. Got some sodding great estate house in the country, a title as well apparently.'

'And "Rubber Balls" Sir?' enquired Bartholomew.

'Never asked.'

The Major rose from his desk. 'I think it's time to rouse the troops and ask some awkward questions, don't you?'

Captain Bartholomew was learning that the Major had a habit of asking him questions that didn't require answers. Major Waller-Boyce walked over to the door that led to the poor excuse for a parade ground and stopping outside on the raised wooden veranda, drew his service revolver and fired three times in the air. The Captain, a little behind, came to a sudden halt and watched the Major as he calmly settled down on the wooden bench and beckoned the Captain to join him, 'Wait and watch Captain, wait and watch.'

Within a few minutes a rag-tag collection of men started to appear in the compound, some running, whilst others just sauntered in at their own pace. A couple even arrived on bicycles and several were in uniform. On seeing the officers, some for the first time, a form of silent panic set in, each man furtively looking at the others for an unspoken explanation.

The Major remained seated, he could feel the Captain holding back the urge to stand up and take charge of the men who had formed a disorderly parade formation in front of them. It was clear this didn't happen often.

After allowing the tension to build, the Major eventually stood up and took a pace forward and lent on the hand rail. He looked at each man in turn for a few moments as if committing their faces to memory. Their collective feeling of unease increased noticeably.

Captain Bartholomew, who was now standing just behind the Majors right shoulder, noted that of the 14 that had attended roll-call that morning, only 26 had presented themselves now!

'Captain Bartholomew here,' began the Major, 'will collect your pay books and I will talk to you all individually. If any of you try to leave the compound the Captain will shoot you for desertion.'

The Major had deliberately spoken slowly, it ensured their complete attention. He also heard Bartholomew behind swallow. Turning to him he said quietly, 'Don't worry Captain I'm sure you won't have to shoot anyone just yet.'

'Thank you Sir.' he replied almost as shocked as the men were. He had to admit, the Major makes his mark very quickly and without shouting, most impressive. That hadn't been in any of the books he'd read at Sandhurst.

Over the course of the next five hours, each soldier was called and interviewed, the Major started with the opening line of . . .

'. . . My name is Major Waller-Boyce, I work for Military Intelligence, I'm a bastard and a thief catcher, I have a bloody good idea of what's been happening here and I don't play ball.' Resting on the desk beside him were two piles of folders, and as he interviewed each he moved a folder from one pile to another. They had nothing to do with the men or the investigation but they didn't know that. He also left his revolver in clear view on the desk - it was unloaded but they didn't know that either.

Waller-Boyce wasn't keen on the bull-in-a-china-shop approach as he called it, but the softly-softly option with these men, some of whom were clearly of lower intelligence, would have been wasted.

It had been an illuminating afternoon for the Major. He had learnt many interesting and often unrelated things about the campsite and the men themselves. Their life here was no-doubt better than anywhere else. Some had set up home outside the camp and enjoyed a freedom like no other. One ran a bicycle repair business, another had a chicken farm, whilst a third ran a makeshift bar and distillery - a challenge in a country of mostly Hindus.

He told each of them not to be taken in by Captain Bartholomew's apparent naiveness, it was all an act and that he was in fact a two faced bastard with the face of an angel who once put a Sergeant in hospital by just shouting at him.

At 16:30, Captain Bartholomew returned to the CO's office and reported that the men were now putting their barracks in order and had started to salute him.

'We seem to be making progress then.' said the Major as he motioned for Bartholomew to sit down, 'Tea?'

'Thank you Sir.' he replied hesitantly.

The Major poured a cup for the Captain and placed it on his desk and then started slowly pacing the room. He always found that people paid more attention if he kept moving, it stopped their mind drifting off elsewhere. He then started to explain what had been going on. It didn't really matter whether Bartholomew was there or not, he just found that running over events out loud helped him think and having someone in the room at the same time meant he wasn't seen as talking to himself.

Withers, the Acting CO, it turned out, hadn't been there for years, no one was quite sure when he was last seen. The goods that did arrive, be it now infrequently, were signed for by the cook, the only one who fitted the old CO's smaller uniform. He also signed the destruction orders, but of course nothing was really destroyed - it was 're-purposed to the greater good,' a mantra coined and instilled by Withers' himself. This 'greater good' was anyone who was prepared to pay for it. The trivial stuff was traded locally whilst the more valuable assets were sent to organised black-market syndicates across India. The clever part from what Waller-Boyce could gather, was the money side - it didn't exist. All transactions were funded and paid for from a central point with the whole affair run like a business avoiding sticky fingers along the line, a common source of weakness in cash-based organisations. This is what pained Waller-Boyce, Withers just didn't have the acumen to run something on that scale, there had to be someone else. It was even more worrying that this may just be one branch of a even larger organisation.

'It's not still going on is it?' asked Captain Bartholomew who raised himself slightly out of his chair to cast a glance towards the camp entrance.

Major Waller-Boyce shook his head in despair. 'No Captain it is not.'

He resumed his thoughts out loud. Withers disappeared around five years ago, as soon as he heard Major Stonely was planning an audit visit. Since then, the camp has just ticked over all by itself.

'Major Stonely didn't find anything wrong then, at the time?'

'No apparently not.' It was said in a voice that didn't quite believe itself.

'So Withers is the key to all this you're saying?'

'Key, as in something that opens a door, yes. He's probably back in England under an assumed name running some seedy night club somewhere.'

'Well I've got a report to write.' finished the Major having strolled over to the door and was holding it open. Moments later Captain Bartholomew got the message and said he also had a few things to do and strode out. As he got halfway across the parade ground Major Waller-Boyce called out 'Try not to shout at the men Captain, they've had a hard day.'

'No Sir.' answered the Captain, somewhat perplexed.

The report wouldn't be an easy one to write; one acting Commanding Officer AWOL, three trucks missing and God knows what else. The only thing he was comfortable with was the almost certain knowledge that the old rifles and ammunition that were stored here had been destroyed or 'repurposed' and not sold on intact to any restless factions. He was holding the small wooden elephant carving he'd bought from the bazaar, it was made from common English walnut, not native to India. The brass and copper had been sourced much closer to hand.

Captain Bartholomew was, as the Brigadier mentioned, here to tidy up and close the camp down, but Waller-Boyce still had the feeling he'd been picked to act as some sort of mentor to this young inexperienced officer - he had to make sure that didn't last.

His report, as detailed as it needs be, pointed the finger squarely at Withers and that the men who remained, four of which were still unaccounted for, blindly followed instructions and certainly shouldn't be punished for that.

Waller-Boyce also recommended that the camp remain operational for as long as possible, pointing out that the present incumbents were there because no-one else wanted them and praised the far-sightedness of the army in placing its problems in one place where the least damage could occur.

Major Waller-Boyce went on to suggest that Captain Bartholomew be the new acting CO, "An ideal platform for a young officer and a position of early responsibility", and one that would keep him out of harms way, i.e. his own.

Major Waller-Boyce made no mention of his suspicions that this was just a small slice of a much bigger pie. Without Withers, he had nothing. He would spend the rest of his short army career looking for clues that might lead to the real power behind the operation. Pencilled on his blotter was the name Stonely, circled many times.

Chapter 3: Major Stonely goes home

The green Bentley Six convertible glided through the village with its deep, mellow throb. Despite the roof being folded down, Major Stonely scarcely glanced at the village itself. He knew it hadn't changed, it never did.

Ahead, stood the two gatehouses that flanked the entrance to Stonely Hall, each with their respective stone pillars adorned with the family coat of arms – six birds divided by crossed swords. Sadly, they had seen better days and were now barely distinguishable.

The long, white, open gravel drive gently curved up to the Hall itself with its clean-lined portico entrance. The Major drove past and around to the stable block opposite the west wing. Originally a large barn-like structure, it had yielded to the modern motor car with a simple widening of the doors.

The Bentley rolled to a satisfying halt on the cobbled courtyard and the engine faded. All the garage doors were open, making the most of the afternoon sunshine. Henderson was washing what had been his mothers Daimler.

It was a moment he had looked forward to, but at the same time, felt a sort of awkwardness that was hard to explain. Henderson was the old gardener's son and a couple of years older than the Major. As children, they had spent much time together and had developed an almost brotherly bond. That was over 30 years ago. When they had met in the solicitor's office a few days previously, they were on a more formal footing and each knew and held their respective place, but this was different. The Major had come home and Henderson had already proved his worth by supplying the Bentley. Besides, the Major didn't really see himself as the Duke of Stonely, it just wasn't him, he felt he had more respect as a military figure, something earned rather than just handed down.

'Good to see you Denis,' said the Major warmly with his hand outstretched.

'Nice to have you back Sir,' Henderson replied and clasped it firmly. They turned and started walking out of the stable yard at an unhurried pace on to the track that led around the edge of the estate through the woods. The Major was keen to get up to speed on events and Denis Henderson was the man to talk to. He knew he'd not only get the unadulterated facts, but also a valued and honest opinion.

'I assume your father's . . .' paused the Major, leaving the sentence unfinished.

'Yes, about 15 years ago now, he was a good age.' replied Henderson, starting to relax a little.

'And you still have that little cottage down by the stream?'

'Riverside Cottage?, no not for a while, your father thought he could put it to better use by renting it out to gentleman anglers fishing for trout and moved me into number two gatehouse cottage.'

'My God! Next door to Hoghorn!' said the Major, astonished and horrified at the same time. 'That must have cramped your style a bit?'

'Let's just say, my nocturnal activities took a turn for the worse.' They both laughed out loud. The ice had been broken. The Major had wanted to renew their friendship but felt his position would create a social barrier and although he was prepared to drop it, he wasn't sure if Henderson would - it looked as though he might.

'I'm in the room above the garage now,' continued Henderson. 'When your father passed away, your mother offered me the use of the space, she knew how stifling Hoghorn could be and I was on the verge of leaving.'

'Thank God you didn't. Is the cottage still rented out?'

'You father leased it to Smallpott just before he died.'

'Bastard' said the Major, almost spitting it out.

Henderson wasn't sure if the Major meant his father the previous Duke or Smallpott, probably the latter. The old Duke had been a shameless tyrant at times and drove people hard but that was his military background, expected for a man in his position. He controlled not just the estate but also owned much of the village too and he loved to exercise power.

There was silent contemplation for a while as they strode on through a wooded area and approached the old boat house.

'Remember Rosie and Doreen?' said the Major as he opened the door and walked inside.

'Oh yes, that was the first time you . . .' Henderson paused.

'Had it off?' finished off the Major.

'I was going to say learnt to swim' laughed Henderson. The Majors mood had lightened. He offered Henderson a cigarette and they both sat down on the old wooden bench inside, looking out at the wide ornamental lake before them.

It had been a hot August evening back then, Rupert Stonely and Denis Henderson had been sitting on that very same bench having a cigarette. 'Can you swim?' asked Denis, Rupert answered that he couldn't. 'Then I shall teach you, strip off'. Rupert was a little stunned but Denis was already undressing. Shyly, he slowly stripped off; he could hear Denis wading out into the cool water. 'Come on, you ain't got nothing I ain't got,' he laughed. Rupert entered the water quickly to cover his naked embarrassment. For the next half-hour, Denis taught him how to float, doggy-paddle and generally 'get the idea' of swimming. There was some touching as Denis supported him, it was unavoidable and Rupert wasn't used to physical contact, shaking hands was as far as that went.

'You boys coming out then' said a voice from the bank. Two girls stood looking at the boys in the water.

'Rupert, may I introduce Rosie and Doreen from the village' said Denis with a broad grin on his face. Rupert stood up, it was the polite thing to do whenever in the company of females his mother had always taught him. He suddenly realised they were in the shallows and quickly put his hands over his 'down-belows.'

The girls giggled, 'Well, if you're not coming out then we'd better come in'. That day was Rupert's 15th birthday and Denis had given him his best present ever.

Henderson leaned forward and rested his elbows on his knees thoughtfully, allowing wisps of smoke to slowly curl upwards in the still air.

'Never did find Doreen's knickers did we?' he said eventually. The Major looked at him and burst out laughing.

'I hid them.'

'Where?'

'Christ, let me think' answered the Major looking thoughtfully at the wooden floor. 'You know, I think I took them with me when I left, memento sort of thing.' Both smiled.

Cigarettes finished, they got up and carried on walking around the grounds, no longer two mature men, but two young lads on a summer's day without a care in the world between them, laughing and joking.

They were almost at full circle and approaching the two gate house cottages. Number one was where Hoghorn lived, a grace and favour accommodation. Despite it being painted white, it still radiated a sense of foreboding. The second cottage, a mirror image of the first, seemed by comparison bright and cheerful.

'You know, I'm still sure she's a bloody witch' said the Major as they passed. They turned and walked up the gravel drive towards the front of the house. The Hall had seen better days. It was shabby and lacklustre but still stately in its own way. The grounds, the Major had noted, were perfect. Henderson saw to that, he was also the odd job man as the Major was to learn later on. His mother, according to Henderson, had become somewhat of a recluse, she lived the last years of her life just in the east wing. The rest of the Hall had been put into mothballs and covered in dust sheets. It was a practical move that made sense at the time.

They reached the front door, stopped and shook hands again. 'You know where I am Sir, if you need anything.' said Henderson reverting back to the master and servant position. The Major understood, best to keep the right formality when others may be able to observe, it wouldn't look right otherwise. The Major continued up the steps to the front door, it wasn't locked and strode in. It took a moment to get used to the dimmer light inside the large open hallway. There was a girl standing to attention at the foot of the wide stairs leading to the first floor.

'Good afternoon, Your Grace' she said with a slight bob of her knees. 'I've put your bags upstairs in the east wing for you.' she looked nervous, a girl from the village obviously, Hoghorn's housekeeping assistant perhaps?

'Just Sir will do, Miss . . .?'

She hesitated for a moment, 'Mary Peters Sir.' she replied nervously not making eye contact. 'Miss Hoghorn would like to know if you're in for supper Sir.'

'Inform Miss Hoghorn that indeed I am.'

My god he thought, he felt like a guest in his own house which in a way, he was. With that, he proceeded upstairs and into the east wing. He opened the first door, it was his fathers study and exactly as he remembered it. The oak-panelled room was a little reminiscent of his London club. Two dark red winged leather arm chairs stood facing the carved stone fireplace, above which, hung a portrait of his great great grandfather attired in the splendid uniform of a mounted dragoon. His male linage seemed to have been involved in most wars and he wouldn't have been at all surprised if they had started them just for the portraits.

The two internal walls were lined with books, hundreds of books. A few of which were written by his grandfather, who had cut with tradition and become an explorer. It was these books that had led to young Rupert Stonely's downfall.

In the middle of the room was the map table, a huge six-legged dark oak platform where maps could be unrolled in their entirety. Battles had been fought and lost on tables like these. Underneath, were chests that contained the neatly rolled maps and figurines depicting battalions of men cast in painted lead, it was toy soldiers for men. Other than that, the room was sparse. There was little in the way of decoration, the odd bronze bust or statue but nothing that could be called personal, no reflection of the man he called father. He went over to the large south-facing window that overlooked the driveway and sat at the mahogany desk with its dark green leather inset writing surface. His Grandfather had had good taste and liked to display it. The Major rummaged through each drawer in turn. They too contained nothing of real interest. He knew that Makepeace, the solicitor, had removed all the documents and accounts relating to the estate itself, in his position of administrator. What the Major was really looking for, was the diary. He knew his father had one, if not several, he had seen it once when he had entered unannounced as a boy, his father slammed it shut and tore him off a strip for forgetting to knock first, but he caught sight of the word diary on the spine. It would make interesting reading.

There was a knock at the door but as the Major looked up, Hoghorn had already entered, she seemed to move about soundlessly and he wondered momentarily if she was related to old Makepeace.

'Dinner is at 7:30, I finish at 8:30 each evening. I start at 6 o'clock precisely and breakfast will be served at 7 o'clock sharp. I do not work on Monday or Wednesday afternoons. The maid works only in the mornings, except today of course.' with that she left.

The Major stared at the space she had just vacated. Curse that woman, here he was behind a desk that commands respect and she just waltzes in like she owns the place. He had, truth be known, wanted to see how she would address him, he looked forward to a 'Your Grace' or a 'Sir' at the very least and the bitch got away without either, damn her eyes.

Turning his attention back to the desk, he wondered if it had a secret compartment, he felt it should and it would have to be Hoghorn-proof to be of any use. He began running his hand around the decorative carved wooden trim that surrounded the top edge of the desk, far too obvious he thought but worth a try. Next, he removed each drawer in turn, measured its length and inspected the runners, again nothing. The single, wide middle drawer however, held a clue. The back edge was thicker and made of a different very slightly-darker wood. Inspecting the back of the drawer slot revealed nothing out of the ordinary. The Major replaced the drawer, sliding it home smoothly. It came to its natural stop but he continued pushing harder.

The green leather writing surface set within the desk top popped up a fraction with a creak that only leather can make. The Major looked around the room, he knew he was alone but felt like a naughty school boy looking into another pupil's desk. He got up and locked the study door, being cautious to leave the key in place, obstructing any low-level passing eyes.

Back behind the desk, he pushed aside the silver inkwell and brass banker's lamp and gently lifted the lid. Inside was a shallow recess, just deep enough for a book at most, it was empty.

The Major let out a breath he hadn't realised he'd been holding. He felt a little insulted that there was no reward for his endeavours. A secret compartment, should at all times contain a secret; to be devoid of such was just . . . wrong.

He ran his hand around the inside and felt an object just tucked under the edge. It was a key.

There was nothing singularly unusual about it, a normal looking door key in all respects. There was a hint of wear on the leading edge that gave the Major some hope of further development. He put it back inside for safe-keeping and closed the desk lid with a reassuring click.

Breakfast next morning and thankfully Hoghorn was nowhere to be seen. The Major ate in peace and read the paper. He'd planned a good look around the house today and to hopefully locate the door to the mystery key. He knew it wouldn't be easy, given the buildings somewhat staggered history.

Stonely Hall hadn't always been in the valley, it hadn't always been a Hall either. It had started life as a castle that once stood proudly on top of Stonely hill, as solid as the very rock it was purported to rest on, until it fell down one night.

The head of the family seat at that time was Duke Rudwick Stonely, who, having woken early that fateful morning, was in the motions of returning a saddle and bridle he had used that previous evening in the bed chamber. His wife's interpretation of horseplay wavered somewhat from the accepted norm. Struggling with the saddle at the end of the dimly-lit passageway, he was feeling blindly with his foot for the first step that led down the west tower to the armoury two floors below. It was steeper than he recalled as he plummeted into the dark void that had sucked out the towers entire contents, steps and all.

Rudwick Stonely gave the appearance of pausing momentarily on his downward journey as he drew level with the ground floor, where a startled man-servant stood wide-eyed holding an oil lamp. He, having been alerted by a deep low rumble moments earlier, had come to investigate. The servant watched in amazement as his master, naked and seemingly astride a saddle passed by with a look of wonder on his face.

The man-servant waited for a horse to follow before he came to his senses and took off with some haste in the opposite direction.

The Duke continued to jockey on down the hole that would later consume the whole west wing.

'Was the rain what done it.' said Dungson later that day to the soon-to-be-confirmed - widow of the Duke. 'Old mine workings in the hill, closed down years ago mind, but the wood had rotted and something had to give and it did last night, collapsed like a dried-out barrel with no hoops.'

Dungson was considered the local building expert even though his particular skill lay in cesspits, a popular man but no one ever shook his hand.

'Have you found the Duke yet?' she asked, resigned to the fact that he was unlikely to have survived.

'bout an hour ago, we opened up the mine an went in. Having a bit of trouble getting him out, looks like he landed on an iron spike, makes it a bit 'ard getting him round corners.' replied Dungson without a thought of decorum or decency. 'Ain't found the horse yet.' he added.

Now Stonely Hall, as it had become, was nestled in the wooded valley between the village and the foot of the hill. Its appearance had changed slightly, well dramatically really. The man in charge of rebuilding the castle in a safer place was named Dungbury, a distant relation of Mr. Dungson who had sadly drowned when he fell into one of his own cesspits. It was the way he'd have wanted to go everyone agreed so they left him there, it was easier.

It had taken over a year to dismantle and number each stone, block and brick, a further five years to cart it down to its new position and rebuild.

Reconstruction had been haphazard at best, most of the labourers were innumerate to start with and when faced with numbers bigger than the varying amount of fingers they owned between them, resulted in a building that resembled little of the original majesty of the castle. Of the 4,000 bricks and blocks left over, most were worked in to the fabric of the village itself, hidden in plain view. It wasn't every baker's shop that had a portcullis arch for a back door.

Now, generations later, the Hall stood more comfortably in the grounds with its rebuilt Georgian-style outer face. Internally it was a mixture of medieval, gothic and Victoriana, it was rumoured there were still rooms without doors and chimneys without fireplaces. There were 23 rooms on a good day.

Chapter 4: The Stonely Secret

Major Stonely was looking forward to exploring his old home with all its little quirks and oddities. It had been over thirty years since he had last set foot inside and wondered if he should be feeling some sort of affection for the place, nostalgia perhaps.

Most homes had a smell that triggered ancient memories, the sound of music, laughter, the waft of freshly-cut flowers sadly, Stonely Hall had none, just beeswax. The male line had always been one of formality and order, it lacked any sort of personality. Being an only-child he had, to some extent, been suppressed by it all, a child's exuberance stifled by its very surroundings. His fondest memories of home life were those spent at boarding school.

Having already familiarised himself with the study, he looked more closely at his fathers bedroom, where he now slept. He had dismissed the ground floor while Hoghorn was about.

The room was sparse and contained no more than was really necessary, just a chest of drawers and a wardrobe, both of which were empty, as was the bedside table. A couple of ornate-framed oil paintings decorated the walls, depicting colourful cavalry scenes. The Major looked behind each, there was nothing. He had reasoned that a man such as his father, stiff and starchy as he appeared, had secrets, a weakness, something personal, maybe even intimate, tucked away somewhere. If he did, he had kept it well hidden.

The door in the corner of the room led to the dressing room and combined bathroom. Again, there were no personal effects, no razor, no badgers-hair shaving brush or comb; it was almost as if he hadn't existed.

A shared door between there and his mother's bedroom had no lock, but an old marble wash stand on an equally heavy cast-iron frame, had been pushed in front of it. That gave a clear message.

His mother's room was almost the opposite, it exhibited typical Victorian tastes in dark wood and lace. The many empty vases were evident of a more feminine aspect. The most dominant feature was the four-poster bed, hung with heavy deep red velvet drapes; it had probably seen little action during his parents marriage. For a moment, he wondered if Smallpott and his mother had done it there, it was a high bed and Smallpott would have had to take a running jump at it. The very thought of a flabby pink penguin-like creature dashing naked across the floor, leaping up and grappling to get a grip on a sliding eiderdown, brought a smile to the Majors face, despite how unsavoury the situation.

It was also the first time he had noticed just how racy the room was. The fire mantle was held up by two naked bronze male figures with no thought of a fig leaf between them. The twin bedside lamps mirrored these images but had brass switches where one would have thought unusual but not totally inappropriate. The Major looked up, hoping against hope that there wasn't a mirror fastened to the underside of the canopy, thankfully not but he did spot the metal rings at the top of each post that weren't there to hold the drapes in place. He was looking at a side of his mother he didn't want to see, it was time to leave.

The last room in that wing was at the back of the house where his mother spent her last days by the look of it. It was cheerful. Overlooking the garden and furnished with tapestries and chintz, it was light and airy, he could well imagine his mother just whiling away the hours looking out on the garden vista. It appeared to contain nothing phallic.

The rest of the upper floors were as Henderson had implied. Dust sheets covered the furniture and paintings and the curtains partially drawn, creating a slightly eerie atmosphere of abandonment. There were hints here and there of better times, the unmistakable shape of a piano in the music room, a covered harp, music stands that stood like frozen players waiting for the conductors opening stroke. Despite all this, he had found no locked door waiting to be opened.

After lunch, he watched Hoghorn walk in her noiseless fashion down the gravel drive to her gatehouse cottage. He relaxed a little, knowing that he was home alone.

When his father had died, he was unable to return to England because of the various uprisings and local unrest or so he had said in his letters home. He wouldn't have been missed. This applied equally to him as it did his father.

His mother understood and wrote of the funeral which was well-attended. Probably to make sure he was dead, the Major suspected. A large tomb was placed on top of the grave for added assurance. His mother's letters, which were at best infrequent, spoke little of Reginald Smallpott at first but over time, it was clear he started to feature more strongly. It was also obvious to the Major, that a relationship had formed, one that was perhaps just spiritual at first but seemed to be growing.

The first mentions were more by-the-bys, Mr. Smallpott called today for tea, but as time progressed, it became Reginald this, Reginald that, Reginald took me for a drive. "He does make me smile and he's so full of life." became a progressive theme. Just how much "life" was Reginald putting in his mother, he had begun to wonder. It was the classic ingratiating rouse, becoming friendly, dependant and trustworthy, all a means to an end and likely as not financially driven. He'd seen it all before and found it distasteful to dwell on, but the Major took comfort that even his mother wouldn't put the family heritage at any risk, He had dismissed the relationship as little more that a woman's flirtation. There was nothing he could do, he was stuck in India.

The Major's army career had been drab to say the least, or so he had engineered it. At first, he showed great promise and rose up the ranks with relative ease. He had reached Lieutenant Colonel through hard work, guile and a touch of blackmail only to be demoted back to Major when he was caught having it off with two rather rotund women who unfortunately belonged to the Major general, one by birth and the other by marriage. It wasn't the first time either. The major recalled the worst 'incident' vividly.
. .

. . . Gerald Hampton-wick, Brigadier, had spent the evening at a ceremonial dinner in the officer's mess. His wife however, made her usual excuse of a nagging headache and remained at home. She had always found these things tediously formal and protracted.

The Brigadier himself, rather unusually, decided to forgo the normal port and cigars and left early to hobble home to his quarters, his gout was starting to get the better of him. Looking resplendent in full uniform he quietly let himself in. The hall light had been thoughtfully left on. Taking off his cap and placing it down on the hall table, he started to undo his belt buckle as he approached the bedroom, being cautious not to make too much noise.

Just as he entered the darkened room silhouetted by the light behind him, he paused inside the doorway letting his eyes adjust. There before him, he could make out a hairy naked pink bottom rising and falling, it was riding the brigadier's rather plump wife.

'By God, have at you Sir!' exclaimed the Brigadier as he struggled to draw his ceremonial sword. Never had the term sabre rattling been so apt.

Stonely, having the advantage of being used to the dim light, quickly made a tactical withdrawal and attempted to hook up his battledress trousers whilst keeping his face away from the brigadiers, for fear of recognition.

The Brigadiers wife remained stunned, lying naked and spread eagle on the matrimonial bed. Stonely grabbed his beret from the bedside table and with his trousers still at half-mast, attempted to throw himself out of the open bedroom window.

The brigadier, by this time, had managed to draw his sword from its scabbard and commenced a charge reminiscent to that of the light brigade, only to be thwarted by his own trousers which had fallen down. He fell headlong onto the bed across his wife who was momentarily winded. The sword, however, found its target and pierced Stonely's retreating scrotum.

The pain was searing and landing in the rose bushes below the bedroom window, did little to help. Not having time to assess the damage, he hobbled into the shadows, his mind drawing an image of the brigadier leaping out of the window in hot pursuit intent on adding Stonelys testicles to his trophy collection.

'Gerald' squealed the brigadier's wife 'Your flag pole's up!' The brigadier looked down to see an old friend that had been decommissioned for a while.

'By God old girl, brace yourself! The cavalry's coming.' and leaped between his wife's open legs.

'Keep your boots on!' she screamed in delight.

Stonely, meanwhile, had managed to dress himself on the run and headed for his quarters. Each step became more painful as the excitement of the moment started to wear off. He needed a doctor, and quickly.

'It's half past bloody two in the morning, can't it wait?' said Major Bates the camp doctor, through the half open window.

'I've just had my balls cut off, for Christ's sake' whispered Stonely in an almost falsetto voice.

'Well it certainly sounds like it,' he smiled, 'Come on in.' Stonely staggered his way up the steps and into the doctors office that was attached to the infirmary. He eased himself on to the examination table and removed his trousers painfully.

'How the hell did you manage that then?' asked the doctor examining Stonely's testicles from a distance.

'I fell into a rose bush.'

'More like you were shagging the brigadier's wife' laughed the doctor.

'Now why would you think that?' grimaced Stonely.

'Well the condom's a fair clue I would say,'

'Bugger.'

The doctor gave him a local painkilling injection and examined his testicles carefully with the occasional 'mmm' and 'ah' thrown in.

'Well it's bad news I'm afraid, we'll have to operate to save your balls old chap.'

'Save 'em, what's wrong with them?'

'They've parted company with your Vas Deferens.'

'And in English?' asked Stonely.

'Think of a conker on a piece of string, now cut the string.'

'Both of them?'

'Yes, we might be able to get a blood flow back to them but the chance of normal sperm production is . . . slim.'

'Can you do it?'

'Good God no, this is a specialist job.' the doctor answered.

'What's the alternative?'

'Alternative, are you mad?'

'Look, I'm not bothered about children, but this has to be just between you and me, I've got to keep this quiet.'

'I see, the brigadier didn't see your face then?' said the doctor. Stonely half-smiled and half-winced.

'Well if you're not bothered about offspring, we can just remove your nuts and stitch up the sack, same as neutering a cat really, you'll still be able to get an erection but you'll be shooting blanks.'

'Will it turn me in to a Jessie?' a worried look spread across Stonely's face.

'God no, to all intents and purposes, you'll be perfectly normal, you'll just have an empty sack.'

'You mean literally, don't you?'

'Yes.' replied Major Bates.

'Can't you put something else in there instead, if I'm seen with no balls, think of the bloody nick-names the men will make up.'

'What would you suggest I use, pickled onions?' asked Bates.

'Are you serious?'

No, you'd get a hard-on every time you ate a cheese sandwich.' said the doctor, almost doubling up with laughter.

'That was a joke wasn't it?'

'Sort of.' he replied, trying not to laugh anymore.

'Ping-pong balls?' suggested Stonely.

'Nope, to large and they'd crush.'

'Ball bearings?'

'Rust.'

'Plum stones?'

'They'd rot.'

'Checker-board pieces?'

'Would have to be ivory.'

'I give up.' said Stonely, defeated.

'I know, golf balls,' said the doctor.

'Far too large, I'd never be able to cross my legs.'

'No, not the whole things, inside, there's a smaller rubber ball, had one split on me the other day, I took it apart to see what was inside.'

'Have you got a couple handy?'

'Of course.'

By 5 am, Lieutenant Colonel Stonely was on his way back to his quarters, very slowly. The operation had been a success, although he felt he was dragging a ships anchor behind him. He'd arranged with the doctor to be sick for a couple of weeks with recommended bed-rest. It had cost him dearly, not just his testicles but also a case of whiskey. It was a price worth paying but sadly short-lived.

Almost six months had passed since the event when he was summonsed to the Brigadiers office.

'My daughters pregnant, what have you got to say?'

'Congratulations Sir.'

'Congratulations - you're the father damn it,'

'Not possible Sir.'

'And why not?'

'I can't reproduce, medical problem Sir.'

'Bollocks.' shouted the Brigadier.

'Precisely Sir, I've not got any, Major Bates will confirm.'

'They felt alright to me!' interrupted the Brigadiers daughter who had been sitting unseen at the back of the room.

'Balls Sir,'

The Brigadier whose face had been going through variations of scarlet now reached vermillion red.

'How dare you speak to my daug . . .'

'Rubber balls Sir, implanted six months ago.'

Stonley had a feeling he had just jumped out of the proverbial frying pan and into the fire.

'Clarissa, leave the room.' ordered her father. The Brigadier now knew it wasn't just his daughter the Stonely had been bouncing his balls off.

An hour later, Lieutenant Colonel Stonely found himself standing to attention before the Major General with the Brigadier in attendance. The meeting had been thankfully brief.

As Stonely emerged from the building, he found Major Bates waiting outside.

'Look, I'm sorry but they had me over a barrel Sir,' said Bates, 'What happened?'

'Demoted to Major.' said the now Major Stonely.

'Christ, sorry to hear that,'

'And being sent to India.' he added.

Major Bates said nothing; he himself was to be posted elsewhere in the country but retained his rank, but thought it best not to mention this, salt-in-the-wound sort of thing. As they walked away, laughter was heard from within, and possibly the words 'Rubber balls.'

With demotion, came suffering. He had broken an unwritten rule and word got around amongst the upper echelons of command. He found himself in charge of army supplies and sent around the country, inspecting stores and stock levels, approving movement of anything from boot laces to trucks, he was, in essence, an auditor with pips on his shoulders. His life of relative comfort was swapped for that of a near nomad.

It hadn't taken the Major long to turn this to his advantage. Being a non-body within, he discovered that things could be lost and manipulated through creative paperwork, people signed for things without actually counting or even looking. He developed a small ring of army personnel who weren't averse to making a few pounds from a misguided case of whiskey or boxes of cigarettes here and there, nothing spectacular, all low key and easily lost. He also discovered he could move around with relative ease. Once he travelled to Ceylon from India through military channels completely unquestioned, he just had to use his - 'don't even consider talking to me' - face. He was good at it.

It wasn't the money that drove him, although it helped, it was the challenge, the 'cocking-a-snoop' at authority that pleased him.

His system had grown and developed to such an extent he found himself, or rather the fictitious company he had formed, supplying surplus to the army itself. He rented out old WWI rifles for training. He was now the head of 'Global Trading-Asia,' it only existed on paper of course, but the people were real, ex-soldiers and dodgy quartermasters had been the backbone of the operation and the cashless payment system he had instigated ensured no one got greedy, redeemable tokens were the order of the day. Some money was invested to provide a special pension from a central fund in the form of shares, they even supplied loans. His greatest achievement, had been with a corrupt minor officer called Withers who ran a storage depot in Northern India, here surplus goods were sent for storage, decommissioned and eventually destroyed on site. Withers just recycled them back into the chain and of course, they ended back at the depot again, it was easier than printing money. Major Stonely welcomed him into the fold.

The Major had never met Withers and only stumbled across his existence in paperwork. In fact he was cautious to never meet anyone who 'worked in the inner circle' for him, it was important that no connection should be made.

Like many things in life, it came to an abrupt end. Someone in Internal Military Intelligence had got wind of it and ironically he had been asked for his assistance in checking the books of various suspect depots, he was briefed by sealed orders from the unseen Major Waller-Boyce who headed the investigation. It was a useful situation which gave him an insight as to what they were looking for. Major Stonely almost burst out laughing when he was asked to visit Pongee and Withers. He'd always wanted to meet him and under the guise of an audit inspection was ideal, Withers didn't know who Stonely really was. Withers, on the other hand, knew who Waller-Boyce was - word had spread. By the time Major Stonely got to Pongee, Withers had done a runner. Stonely 'cleaned up' the books to make sure he himself wasn't implicated.

His memories were interrupted by the echo of a door banging closed downstairs. He looked out the window to see the maid crunching down the drive, he had forgotten about her. Now he really was alone.

Like a pubescent teenager waiting for the right time to do something naughty in his bedroom, he opened up the secret desk compartment and withdrew the key.

He wondered if it just might be some sort of master key, he had assumed it was a door key, it seemed too large for a chest or clock case. He decided to try it on the study door. Removing the original key he slipped it in, it fitted and turned smoothly. There was an audible clunk and this was followed by a creaking sound off to his right. Looking around the study, he saw that a section of the bookcase had swung open, revealing a dimly-lit hollow behind. He looked back at the key in the door and unlocked it, the bookcase remained open. How clever, he thought, a secret door that only opened when the study door was locked. With the study door once again secured, he went over to the open bookcase and stepped inside.

He found himself midway on a very narrow, stone, spiral staircase. Natural light was filtering in from somewhere above, giving just enough illumination to encourage him to go down.

He had only taken a few steps, when he saw the little alcove in the wall, he drew in a breath. Here were his father's diaries. The Major found himself torn between reading them back in the comfort of the study or pressing on and seeing what lay at the bottom of the stairs. Curiosity won the battle between comfort and exploration.

The stairs stopped abruptly on the ground floor. The space ahead of him was a bricked-up doorway that he guessed used to come out under the main stairs. The Major had expected it to lead down to the cellar, which it clearly didn't, He started to form an idea that these were originally the servants' back-stairs and at the top end would be their quarters in the attic. As he turned to investigate upstairs, his foot snagged with something metal on the floor. It was an iron ring set in a large wooden trap-door which had blended in with the dusty floor.

Chapter 5: Hidden Depths

'It's a hole,' said Henderson, peering down the black void before him.
'I know it's a bloody hole,' replied the Major.
'And you want to know what's down there, don't you?'
'It would help, yes.'
'And you want me to find out, I suppose?'
'It would help, yes.' repeated the Major smiling.

When he first discovered the wooden trap-door it was akin to those boyhood adventures he had read at boarding school, hidden under the bed covers. They inevitably involved treasure or smugglers, or rather predictably both. What always featured, was a friend who came to the rescue at the last minute when the hero got caught, and so the Major had to rein in his natural urge to explore and err on the side of staying alive and Denis Henderson was the nearest he had to a real friend.

Henderson carefully tied the rope on to an iron ring set in the wall and eased himself down the hole.

'You won't leave me down here if the rope breaks will you?'
'Of course not - who'd mow the lawn?'

Whenever the two of them got together, it was almost as if they were simply carrying on from where they left off all those years ago as childhood playmates.

The Major watched him slide down the rope and land on the dirt floor below.

'Oh my God!' called out Henderson as he stood there, illuminated by the Majors torch from above.

'What can you see?'
'Nothing, I haven't turned my torch on yet.'
'Bastard'
'Probably.' replied Henderson with a laugh.

After a few moments, the top of a wooden ladder poked out of the hole.

'You can come down now, it's your turn to hide.' called out Henderson from below.

Tentatively, the Major descended the wooden ladder until he was on firm ground. He flicked on his torch and shone its dust-laden beam around. It revealed what seemed to be a large laundry room.

'Looks like a large laundry room.' said Henderson.
'I was just thinking that.' replied the Major.

It was difficult to get a full picture by torch light alone but they could make out large wooden tubs and pipes, lots of pipes. The earthen floor implied that this wasn't purpose-built but the surrounding walls were solid stone, these could only be the foundations of the original Hall, thought the Major.

'A laundry with no door?' said Henderson eventually after having traced the contours of the room.

'And a fireplace with an oven.' added the Major.

'Baking bread in a laundry, I can't see that somehow.'

'Unless. . .' paused the Major. He dropped to one knee and started picking up small grains from the floor. Henderson shone the torch into the Majors open hand.

'Wheat?' said Henderson, 'for bread.'

'Barley' replied the Major, 'for beer.'

'You can't surely mean. . .' said Henderson leaving the sentence unfinished.

'It's not a laundry, it's a bloody brewery!' smiled the Major in triumph.

Both men were familiar with brewing beer, for different reasons. Henderson, because it was part of country life and Stonely, because he had helped supply the necessary equipment to some very grateful troops back in India.

They wandered around examining the tubs, it certainly made sense. The pipes heated from the fire that lead to a large covered cauldron and from there to the first tub for mashing, the second for fermentation and the third for maturing. The oven, of course, roasted the barley; it was home brew on a large scale.

'It still needs a proper door.' mumbled Henderson.

Later that afternoon, Henderson busied himself down in the brewery whilst the Major went for a walk around the outside of the Hall. The cellar had two entrances, one via the kitchen and the other, a set of thick double doors on the side of the east wing. Hoghorn always locked the scullery entrance.

Armed with a key from Henderson, the Major opened the first door with ease but the second hadn't moved for years and offered some resistance at first. He needed both open wide enough for light to spread inside. That done, he walked cautiously down the stone ramp.

The brewery roof had been curved, he recalled, but the cellar roof above was a vaulted affair similar to that of a church crypt, clearly an indication of different building phases. Thick stone pillars were regularly placed to support the building above, creating a labyrinth feeling. Somewhere near the middle, he found the steps that led to the scullery above and searched for the light switch. It had little effect; it merely increased the depth of the shadows.

The Major was trying to remember what he knew about the cellars. He had never been allowed down there as a child and it had been rumoured that his ancestors were entombed within its depths, probably to discourage him from trying.

What it really held was junk, well not perhaps junk as such, more like surplus furniture that had fallen in or out of favour, dependent on which generation were resident at the time.

He recognised his Grandfathers battered travelling-trunk as well as his military campaign desk that had been superseded by his fathers in the drawing room, and low and behold, the seed cabinet from the glasshouse. Moving aside a couple of dusty chairs, he slid open the long, narrow top drawer with its neatly divided compartments, it was empty, as expected. For a moment, it brought back the memory of his sixteenth birthday. He had returned home from his last term at boarding school and was presented with an army cadet uniform and a travelling trunk in the morning and dispatched to military college as a resident student in the afternoon, punishment for his foray into the herbal food market with the village baker. He remembered his mother sobbing on the steps waving goodbye and Hoghorn behind her with the merest hint of a smile on her face. His father wasn't present; he had better things to do apparently.

Snapping back from one gloom to another, he looked around and spotted the wine cellar at the back. A locked iron gate barred his way. He wondered if Makepeace held sway over that too. Slowly orientating himself around, he found what must have been the dividing wall between him and the brewery. It was in semi-darkness and devoid of features. Certainly, there was no trace of a door.

Working his way along, he came across a recessed section of wall between two pillars going back some six feet. At the back, was a long, wide, stone slab and a crudely carved plaque above. Oddly, the stone step had an iron rod sticking out of the middle some three feet tall. Holding on to the top of the rod, which was worn smooth to the touch, he stepped up onto the slab and tried to read the inscription. At best he could just trace out the name . . . Rudvvic.

As he placed one hand on top of the plaque, it moved just a little bit. He nudged it again and grit fell from underneath. Running his fingers around the edge he got a purchase and gently pulled, it swung open with a light grinding noise. Behind was a deep, square hole, he had hoped for a treasure horde but got nothing, it was empty, except for a narrow vertical strip of golden light at the very back. For the slightest of moments he thought he had found the hiding place of the Holy Grail and pushed his hand forward.

A wooden panel fell away and revealed the ashen face of Henderson in the brewery beyond.

'Fuck me, I nearly shat myself!'

Back in the not-quite-comfort of the brewery, Henderson showed the Major where his face had appeared apparition-like before him. The hole on this side had been coved up by a two foot square, wooden board with a couple of coat hooks on it. They now realised they had been used as handles.

'Its still not a door.' said Henderson, after they had each relived their respective experiences from each side of the wall.

Henderson had been busy, he had discovered electricity; well not so much discovered, as re-routed. He'd strung up a light in each corner which gave enough illumination to get a better over-all picture of the brewery.

To say electricity had come late to the village of Stonely, would have been an understatement, it hadn't arrived at all. An early generator had been installed with much enthusiasm in the grounds, but had proved to be so temperamental that it hadn't lasted the week, and was passed on to the village inn, where after much tinkering and grafting of tractor parts it had more good days than bad. The resulting power had been split between the two buildings.

Now under the occasionally flickering light, they could see that the cellar was surprisingly dry and aired, a clue that some care had been taken.

'Any thoughts on how this got here?' asked Henderson as the Major re-examined the walls.

'It can only have been my Grandfather the explorer, he's the only one who had a sense of fun and drank like a fish apparently, I know he had alterations done but no-one really knew what, you could open a cupboard door and discover a bedroom behind it.'

They were coming across more evidence now for the brewery theory. Folded barley sacks and hop heads swept in a corner. A couple of buckets, a wooden oar from the boat house and two pewter tankards seemed to seal its identity.

'I really like to know how they got the bloody barrels out.' said Henderson showing signs of mental frustration.

'I don't think they did.' answered the Major.

Major Stonely was holding a coiled length of canvas-covered rubber hose he had taken down from a hook on the wall. It was the sort used for pumping water. Henderson stepped over and examined the ends: each had a metal collar with an internal thread. Thinking as one, they went to the last vat and looked of a suitable coupling. Sure enough, there it was at the bottom. A sense of excitement started to grip them both; the final solution was at hand.

Carefully screwing one end on, they dragged the other over to the hole in the wall, well almost.

'It won't reach the hole.'

'Had a girl say that to me once.' said Henderson.

The Major looked at him quizzically.

'She had really big thighs.'

'There must be somewhere else?'

'She said that too, very accommodating she was.'

The Major slapped him on the back.

'You don't let things get on top of you do you? no don't answer that,' he laughed.

With the hose at full stretch, they circled the room to establish its reach and stopped at the side of the fireplace. There, just above floor level, was a pipe with an external thread that the hose reached easily.

'The Pipe Line.' remarked Henderson, 'of course.'

'Prey tell?' asked the Major raising an eyebrow.

'Old Hogget's field, it was,' recalled Henderson gazing into the middle distance, 'I remember my father and grandfather talking about it. I asked why the village celebrated Burnt Cow Day every year in Hogget's field and they made up this stupid story, only it wasn't a story, it was true.'

'And?' asked a frustrated Stonely.

'Let me think for a moment, I can piece it together, it started one afternoon back in . . .'

'. . . They're drunk, I tell you' said Jed Henderson.

'The cows are drunk?' repeated Hogget in disbelief.

'Totally pissed.'

'Not just spooked,'

'Oh definitely drunk, one's up a tree.'

Jed Henderson and Hogget made their way over to the field to have a closer look. Sure enough, the cows were out of sorts. Several were following each other around in a circle, another thought it was a sheepdog and had pinned three others into a corner. To one side, several had collapsed in a heap and sure enough, one was straddling the lower branch of an oak tree several feet off the ground - not a bad achievement for a hoofed animal.

Wisely walking around the outer edge of the field, they came across the probable cause. A shallow in the ground was filled with what smelt like beer. This is where the last cow was resting, lying down in the middle, lapping up the beer at one end and evacuating its bowels at the other.

'The bloody pipe's broken, best get the boys together, we've got work to do!' said Jed to farmer Hogget.

It took two days to dig out the sodden mess. The boys, local farmhands, on hearing the news, rushed to the site with shovels, wheelbarrows and as many empty bottles as they could muster: this was an opportunity not to be missed. Hogget told them that it was best not to try and drink the stuff but they just waved him away. He smiled when one said it was the shittiest beer he'd ever tasted.

The old spring water pipe from the hills used to supply water to the Stonely estate and also fed the lake. The overflow was piped down to the village pump in the square for communal use. Over time, it fell into disuse and the hand pump was replaced with a fountain, a copy of the one in the centre of the estate lake, complete with a duplicate bronze casting of Bacchus.

Duke Stonely the 10th, the Majors Grandfather, had come up with the brewery as a way to avoid the beer tax and make a small income, not that Stonely needed it, he felt good just to be able to give something back to the village, it was a fun thing to do in his retirement.

The beer was brewed in a secret brewery. Wheat and hops grown locally, were delivered in one of the Dukes pony and traps, under the seat. The Duchess was oblivious of these arrangements but used to complain of the strange musty smell emanating from the upholstery at times. Most people assumed one of the gatehouse cottages doubled as the brewery, others erred towards Riverside Cottage. No one but a very select few, knew the real truth. It was the Duke himself who came up with the idea to utilise the existing spring water pipe to carry the beer. Originally, it was to terminate at the fountain itself, the idea being that people filled up bottles or jugs as and when and left a donation in the cup Bacchus held in his hand. The profit split between the inn and the estate. The problem was the outlet itself. The statues bronze penis was the obvious choice, being easily within reach but a turn-cock would have to be installed in place of his testicles. The idea was later dropped, when they realised that perhaps farmer's wives and daughters might pick up a bad habit with potentially painful consequences, it didn't paint a pretty picture. A better solution had to be found and that was the village inn itself.

The pipe was diverted and connected to a narrow pipe that ran along under the bar to a tap above the sink. It looked like any ordinary tap and would pass a random revenue inspection. A bonus was, that the beer would sit quite happily in the main pipeline at an ideal temperature and so there was no need for barrels or bottles. The few barrels they had delivered were always legitimate and brewed in the county. And so it was, fresh beer was literally available on tap behind the bar at the Stonely Arms Inn.

Day two of the pipe repair and disaster struck. One farmhand, having worked out a way to filter the beer with his handkerchief and a sock, had consumed far too much and disappeared behind some straw bales that had been used to soak up the beer the previous day and relieved himself. He let his fag end drop and it immediately set fire to the straw which had now dried out in the hot summer sun. The farmhand raised the alarm by running around the field with the front of his trousers on fire. A quick thinking lad who had been using the old portable fire pump to keep the hole drained aimed the hose at the now well-alight straw bales. Unfortunately, Stonely Ale had a higher than usual alcohol content, that when formed into a spray by the pump created a flame-thrower effect and turned a third of the field into stubble. From that day on, it was referred to as Burn Cock field but later changed at the insistence of the local ladies to Burnt Cow Field out of respect for Tommy 'knobless' Pipkins who never fully recovered from the event. A picnic was held annually in his memory even though everyone had forgotten who he was by now. He left no family.

The Major sat fascinated, listening to Henderson slowly piece together the story. Some was guess-work, some was known history. It was certainly true that a picnic was still held in Hogget's field to this day. There would be few left that would ever know the whole story.

'I guess when your Grandfather died, the brewery died with him.' finished Henderson.

'No, I don't think it did.' said the Major.

'Surely your father wouldn't have carried on the, shall we say - family tradition - it just wasn't him.'

'Well that's what I would have thought but I think he did for a while, I discovered some hidden diaries, well more like accounts really, they show payments made for wheat, barley and hop supplies but over time he started buying cheaper supplies from other farms away from the village, income from sales fell. It ceased to be local anymore, people stopped drinking his beer and growing hops, my father just wasn't a people person, he didn't understand how a local economy worked and the whole thing just collapsed and I don't think he ever forgave the villagers, despite it being his own fault. Let's face it, he was a thoughtless bastard.'

Henderson smiled, 'you're not . . .'

'Like him? No, I know which side my bread is buttered.'

The diaries had been enlightening and clearly showed a declining trade. The Major had hoped to discover an insight into his father's personal life, his thoughts and ambitions but there were none. The odd mention here and there of cryptic purchases and sales bemused Stonely. £200 received for a 'bastard' and a quantity of equestrian supplies totalling some £180 which was odd - his father hated horses.

The two of them sat in quiet contemplation for a while.

'Seems such a shame, all this is wasted' said Henderson finally breaking the silence. The Major looked at him and smiled. They were both thinking the obvious.

'Brewing beer is just impractical, were old men now, it just wouldn't work.' said Henderson.

'No, you're right, totally impractical, wouldn't work, the labour involved well, we just couldn't do it, as you say, we're not young men anymore and I wouldn't trust anyone else.

'And the pipe probably has more leaks that a knitted bucket.' added Henderson.

'Even if we could, there's little chance the current landlord would be obliging.' said the Major.

'Oh, Clifford's OK, he's the good old sort, he'll be interested.'

'Still, even if we could brew beer, it might be just awful.' ended the Major.'

'Can't be much worse than the local brewery, we're on Bishops Nipple' at the inn.

'Well I suppose it's got spirit at least' laughed the Major. He stopped and looked at Henderson.'

'Spirits.' they both said together.

Chapter 6: True Spirit

They both agreed that the distillery was a brilliant idea and far more practical for their collective abilities.

'Christ, we could knock-up a batch in the afternoon, bottle it and have it down the pub by the evening.' said Major Stonely, rubbing his hands together.

'Don't even have to bottle it, we could use the pipeline,' added Henderson with equal enthusiasm.

'Do you think it still works?'

'Only one way to find out.'

They sat and thought for a while and probably came to the same conclusion; best not to jump the gun just yet.

'We'd have to talk to Clifford.'

'You say we can trust him?' asked the Major.

'Oh yes, he's as bent as a nine bob note.'

'Fancy a pint this evening?'

'Already there.' smiled Henderson.

That evening, the Major selected his second-best tweed jacket and waistcoat. He was keen to give a squire-like impression but still imply he was a man of the land, but didn't actually plough it. Informing Hoghorn that he would be dining out, he set off down the gravel drive towards the inn. It was time to meet Clifford and the locals.

The village square broadened before him, it was an odd feeling. The last time he had walked that way, he had been a school boy and it was exactly the same. The bakery and tea shop where he once sold his 'herbs', hadn't changed and the fountain was still there. He was surprised it hadn't been melted down to help out the war effort, but then again, his father had so much influence that he could have more or less ensured the Village of Stonely didn't exist, if he wanted it that way.

He entered the inn, ducked the low beam expertly and strode purposely over to the bar.

'Clifford isn't it?' asked the Major to the man behind the bar.

'Yes Sir' he replied hesitantly, he quickly realised this stranger had an air of authority and, dare he think it, class.

'Duke of Stonely', said the Major offering a hand.

'Your Grace' replied Clifford somewhat stunned and very slightly honoured.

'Just Major will do, not keen on titles myself.' he replied, contradicting himself.

'Well . . . Major, what can I get you?' said the slightly more relaxed Clifford.

'Bishops Nipple I believe is the order of the day, and refills for the chaps in the corner.'

There was a murmur of approval from the shadows with a hint of "gov'ner" thrown in.

'I understand you do food?' he asked as Clifford poured his pint.

'Yes, limited menu of course, what with rationing and all. Mostly mutton stew actually.' Clifford was starting to squirm.

'The sort with feathers?' said the Major in a low voice looking past the landlord. Clifford's eyes followed his to the floor behind him.

'I'm not a game keeper Clifford, but I know pheasant feathers, the smell of poached salmon and recognise a smokehouse in the trees when I see one.' said the Major to a now pale-faced Clifford.

'You can't fool the Major, Clifford' said Henderson who had now appeared alongside him at the bar.

'Welcome home Major,' said Clifford, 'may I recommend the salmon.' he knew when he was beaten.

The Major and Henderson enjoyed a good supper, They had declined the use of the more private dining room and sat instead at a window table in the bar.

Slowly, the inn started to see more people drift in. Word had spread that the new Duke was in residence and he appeared to be quite friendly, the curious came to see for themselves.

By 9 o'clock, it was by village standards, busy. Clifford was happy, he knew it was going to be short-lived but he was going to make the most of it. Bishops Nipple had run out and had been replaced with the more popular Stag Stout with its merest hint of venison which always improved the sale of cold meat sandwiches.

'Mr. Richards' said Henderson, rising from his seat. The Major looked up to see a man as old as an oak and twice as gnarled.

'Mr. Richards is Clifford's Grandfather, one of the earlier landlords,' said Henderson with a wide smile. 'And this Mr. Richards, is Major Stonely, the new Duke.'

'Bastard.' said Mr. Richards.

The pub went quiet. The Major stayed looking at him expressionless.

'Never liked the old one, full of shit.' said Mr. Richards. The Major laughed and the tension was broken. Glasses that had frozen in mid drink, finished their journey to their respective owner's mouths.

The Major and Henderson spent the rest of the evening talking to Richards and his equally ancient friends; there was information for the gathering.

At closing time, which was normally when the last person left, rather than the ringing of a bell, the Major and Henderson were shown the cellar by Clifford who hadn't until then known the history of the pipeline and was keen to find out more.

Mr Richards the elder, who being of a somewhat fragile nature was gently lowered, tied to a chair, into the cellar via the outside delivery chute. Under his direction, a mirror above the small sink was unhooked, revealing a faint circular stain on the wall. Clifford chipped away at the damp plaster with the claw end of a hammer, exposing the end of the pipe recessed a couple of inches below. The wooden bung was still in place. With some effort, the plug was removed with a pop, followed by a trickle of muddy water. Clifford opened a bottle of special reserve, the good stuff and stories were exchanged well into the night.

The next afternoon in the brewery, the Major and Henderson waited patiently with a gallon of water and a funnel. It was Clifford's idea to test the pipeline in the most practical way, trial by fire but with water, obviously.

The Majors pocket watch chimed three and pouring began.

At the inn, Clifford waited equally patiently in the cellar with a bucket and mop. The water began its journey down the pipe. This would be repeated at fifteen minute intervals until four o'clock.

The first three were to flush the pipe out and hopefully the last, to measure how much was lost. By 4pm Clifford was looking at less than half a gallon of muddy water in the bucket. It wasn't good.

Later that evening, Henderson chatted with Cliff about the disappointing results, it had certainly put a damper on their plans.

'At least we know it's still connected,' said Clifford, after they had sat there in silence for a while.

'I think we'd better borrow one of Marvin's ferrets' said Henderson. Clifford smiled, now that was country thinking.

The next evening saw the Major at his most uncomfortable, he hated ferrets. He was all too aware of their habit of latching on to fleshy parts and held it judiciously at arms length. It pissed on him. Fighting back the urge to strangle it, he waited the last few seconds before the eight o'clock release time. It was as pleased to leave him as he was to see it go.

Back at the pub, those in the know, of which there were few, placed bets. Within fifteen minutes, the ferret popped its head out into the cellar of the Stonely Arms. A cheer went up from all but Jake Thackery who lost five shillings.

Over the next couple of days, plans were made. Henderson suggested that a rubber hose was threaded down the pipe and it would be this, that any liquids would pass through. It eliminated both contamination and pickled snails and was better for the smaller volume of spirits compared to the gallons of beer the larger bore had been carrying.

The hose and other sundry supplies, had been purchased on the Stonely account as a legitimate gardening expense and raised no suspicion or curiosity.

Wednesday evening and the Major and Henderson set the ferret off again with some strong twine tied to a small leather harness Henderson had supplied.

'You're very skilled in leatherwork.' said the Major.

'It was Shirley the barmaid really, she's good with her hands.' he winked.

As before, after fifteen minutes, the ferret appeared in the inns cellar, given a nip of beer and returned to its grateful owner. A stronger, thicker cord was tied on to the end of the twine and two hammer taps on the pipe was the signal for the brewery end to start pulling it through.

'Stage one complete, commence stage two.' ordered the Major.

'Stage two commencing Sir.' mimicked Henderson in a humorous mocking tone. If all goes well, it should emerge with the much stronger cord tied to the other end. It did. Henderson then tied the cord around the stopped-up end of the rubber hose securely. Henderson gave the word and the Major tapped three times on the pipe. Operation Enema, as it had been dubbed, was underway.

'This is stupid,' said the Major to Henderson the next morning, as they both sat on the bench in the boathouse.

'It's not, it's a bloody good idea.' rebuffed Henderson.

'No, not the pipeline, I mean me having to come out here to have a cigarette. I can't smoke inside my own home without Hoghorn tut-tutting.'

Henderson smiled, he knew the feeling. 'Did you know she's asked me to get some rat poison?'

'Don't tell me the bitch plans to poison me?'

'No, well maybe not yet, she claims she heard rats under the kitchen floor last night and wants me to put some down the drains.'

'Are there rats?'

'No, she must have heard the hose pipe being dragged through the old pipeline, I told her it was probably rats.'

'Good thinking' replied the Major and added casually, 'What do you know about distilling?'

'Not a bloody thing but I know a man who does.'

'Ideal, we should have a go before we get too far ahead of ourselves don't you think?'

'I shall go and ask questions this very morning, are you thinking of doing it in the cellar?'

'Christ no, if it goes tits up I'd be in deep shit, Hoghorn would love that, no, we'd better find somewhere secluded for the first attempt.'

'Yes you're right, we could do it up Jacks Bottom,'

'Do you think he'd mind?' said the Major in some surprise.

'Jacks Bottom, it's a small ravine in the woods there's a stream and it's close to Riverside cottage and the wood yard, any smoke rising will be mistaken for me burning rotten wood.

'What about Smallpott himself?' enquired the Major.

'He's not been up for a couple of months; we'd know if he was here.'

'Sounds ideal, what do we need?'

The next hour was spent making a mental list.

During the day, Henderson had dropped off various items to be put together that evening with the Majors help.

Jacks Bottom was a shallow crease in the floor of the wood and well hidden, a stream ran into this and dropped down some four feet to the bottom giving a trickling waterfall effect. Henderson had dug out a hollow next to the waterfall and built a small fireplace. Over this, was placed what could only be described as a large kettle.

'We're making tea then?' Joked the Major.

Henderson laughed. 'No, we're going to boil up some apple cider!'

'But that's already got alcohol in it.'

Yes but distilling concentrates it, makes it stronger.'

'So how would we make vodka or whisky then?'

'We'd have to ferment the basic ingredients first for a couple of weeks then distil it.

'Oh.', replied the Major, he was obviously disappointed. 'I was hoping we wouldn't have to do anything like that.'

'Can't be avoided I'm afraid, we'd be limited to small batches but it's still easier than making beer.' Henderson hoped this was some small consolation; he was enjoying himself and didn't really want it to end to quickly.

'So, if we were to make, say Vodka, what would we need?'

'Well from what I understand, just potatoes.'

'And Whisky?'

'Wheat or barley,'

'Well that's easy then.' finished the Major now a little happier.

'Ah,' added Henderson, 'Vodka has no taste and whisky needs to mature in decent barrels for a couple of years otherwise no one would by it.

'True,' agreed the Major, 'but if say Clifford were to dilute his existing stock with our flavourless Vodka supply it must surly double his income without affecting its taste?'

Henderson had to agree, it was a good argument. The Major knew it would work, he had arranged a similar thing back in India in the sergeant's mess with the stewards. He was a happier man now.

'Just a thought, what do we do with the waste products?' asked the Major.'

'Pig feed'

'Happy pigs,' they both smiled.

Henderson poured the cider into the kettle, placed the lid back on and packed some wet clay around the top to seal it. On the end of the spout was a short length of rubber hose and to that, he added a coiled length of copper piping which he positioned into the flowing water from the little waterfall above. He lit the fire under the kettle.

'So how does this actually work? This seems a little too simple.' asked the Major who was quite enthralled.

'That's just it, it is. All you're really doing, is boiling up the liquid into steam, it passes along the copper pipe, the water on the outside cools the steam inside and that condenses back into a liquid and dribbles out of the end, that's the distillate, moonshine sort of thing, except with apples.'

'Its apple sweat then?'

'Yes basically,' answered Henderson.

'So you could do that with any fermented fruit then?'

'Yes, except tomatoes, of course.'

Within a few minutes, a clear liquid started to drip from the end of the copper pipe into the tin mug. After another ten minutes, Henderson carefully picked up the now half-full mug and threw its contents into the stream. The Major's mouth just dropped open.

'Best not to use the first few drops, it's contaminated, but from here on in, we should be alright.'

Some twenty minutes later, the fire under the kettle was put out and both eyes turned to the almost-full tin cup.

'After you, Your Grace.' said Henderson, smiling like the proverbial Cheshire cat.

'Oh no Denis . . . after you, I insist.' replied the Major. Henderson took a slow and cautious sip from the mug. He had planned to remain expressionless but couldn't stop a smile coming to his lips. He finally uttered . . . 'Not bad, not bad at all.'

The Major took the cup and tentatively took a sip, he knew Henderson might be having a little joke but until he tasted it he'd not know.

'Bugger me, that's good.'

'No and yes, in that order.' replied Henderson.

The two men remained by the still, taking turns with the tin mug, they were both pleased and perhaps even a little surprised that it just worked. Now they had to plan how to scale it up and what to make. The distilled cider had worked well but that would be a more seasonal thing, they needed ingredients that were available all year round, or could be stored and besides, not everyone liked cider.

By the time they had finished the cup, it had been decided that unless they could come up with a completely new drink, Vodka would be the answer.

10 o'clock that evening and the Major was in the boathouse having a cigarette, he was usually joined by Henderson who turned up late but had that smile on his face, smug and very pleased with himself. He sat down on the bench and passed the Major a small bottle of an amber-coloured liquid.

'Go on, try it.'

The major unscrewed the top and gave it a sniff, it had a pleasant aroma that had the warmth of a spirit but the depth of a good brandy.

The taste that hit the major first was almost acidic, like taking a bite out of a lemon but it immediately disappeared to be replaced by a soothing fruity palette soaking sensation of . . .

'Apricots?' asked the Major looking at Henderson.

'And?'

'Peaches I think, it keeps changing.' The Major was now starting to experience something akin to a half descent Brandy. Suddenly he stood up and made a face like a bulldog chewing a wasp.

'Crab apples?' asked Henderson enjoying the Major struggling to keep his composure. 'It will pass.' he assured the him and it did, to be replaced by the brandy again and then it went, not slowly, it stopped dead, leaving a warmth in the chest. The Major sat down and was, well, speechless, quite literally, he mouthed the words but no sound came out, panic started to show in his eyes and Henderson just leaned back on the bench and smiled. The effect only lasted a few seconds but the Major still remained stunned.

'Please tell me you made that.' asked the Major.

'I made that.' replied Henderson.

Chapter 7: Special Brew

Denis Henderson and Major Stonely found themselves, once more, up Jacks Bottom. They sat watching condensation form on the copper coil as the old iron kettle did its work. The first few drops had already come through, landing in the tin mug with a discernable 'plink'. When it reached half-way, Henderson had thrown out the contents and replaced the mug. It seemed sacrilegious but it was for the best - this stuff had the potential to do some serious damage.

The Major examined the three empty bottles Henderson had used to fill the kettle. Two still bore the hand written labels, one declaring rhubarb and the other, blackberry. The third bottle although giving no hint on the outside had a distinct cherry aroma. There was a little left in the bottom and the Major took a swig, immediately spitting it out and wiping his mouth on the back of his hand.

'That was foul.'

'They all are, no-one ever drinks this stuff.' said Henderson with a knowledgeable smile. He went on to explain the history of the wine made by farmer Percy, known locally as Paraffin Percy, but never to his face.

Percy had been making wine from farm produce and hedgerow fruit for more than fifty years. It was purely a hobby, a way to use nature's free bounty, as he always said. So pleased with his handiwork, he presented everyone in the village with a bottle on special occasions such as birthdays, weddings, deaths and days ending with a 'y'. The problem was, no one drank it, they had all tried it of course but the lust for continued wellbeing overrode the desire for an early death. All agreed that it was the most insidious, fermented concoction known to man and beast but it was quite good at getting the soot off paraffin lamps. Percy had always been a well-respected farmer, generous and always willing to lend a hand that no one ever refused his offerings for fear of upsetting him. It wasn't until he was spotted at a local market taking a bite out of an onion, that they realised his sense of taste fell short of the full range.

Percy was dead now but his legend lived on, some people still had the odd bottle or two under the sink, just in case they found a good use for it. Denis Henderson had!

'So distilling improves it?' asked the Major.

'Well it seems to leach the poisons out and brings back the fruit taste, plus giving it a hell of a kick.' smiled Henderson.

This should be interesting, mused the Major, taking a pull on his cigarette.

Enough liquid had now been gathered for a taste but both were a little hesitant to be the first. Bravely, the Major removed the mug and slid one of the empty bottles in its place, just in case it was worth preserving. Tilting the mug, he could see it had a pink hue. Finally, he took a sip and quickly passed it over to Henderson in case he suddenly lost control of his bodily functions.

There was tartness at first, giving over to a fruity, over-ripe blackcurrant essence that was suddenly attacked by an overwhelming cherry brandy Liqueur that coated the entire mouth with a sickly sweet taste that lingered. He watched Henderson's face as he took his turn, he just winced.

'Woman's drink!' they said together. Nonetheless, they finished it off.

The peace was broken by the sound of a car approaching along the distant wooded lane. Both the Major and Henderson knew immediately who it was. Smallpott had decided to spend the weekend at Riverside Cottage. They were a good distance from the cottage, hidden on the most part by the ravine and low foliage but they were well positioned to observe.

Smallpott stopped the car just short of the Cottage, got out and walked around to the back.

'Waddles like a ducks arse,' said the Major.

'Shhhh' hissed Henderson putting his finger up to his mouth and trying not to laugh. It was with some effort, the rather rotund Smallpott eased his case out of the trunk and struggled to lift it with any grace. He returned a few moments later and very carefully removed a large, flat, square blanket-covered package, which he rested on the lip of the boot and started to unwrap. There was a brown paper parcel inside. It was at this moment, that the Major unintentionally but loudly, passed wind.

Smallpott froze, the Major buried his face in the earth and Henderson clamped his hand over his mouth. Smallpott looked around furtively and hurriedly shut the car boot and wobbled quickly into the cottage, clutching his parcel.

Stonely and Henderson dared not look at each other until they had suppressed the urge to laugh out loud. It would appear that 'Ladies Cherry', as they had christened it, was more potent than they had given it credit for.

Moving with great caution, they extinguished the last embers of the fire. The two of them then set off towards the wood yard north of the cottage where they would be able to get back into the estate via the gate in the boundary wall. As they approached the yard, Henderson grabbed the Majors arm and pulled him behind a wood pile.

'I'm not that sort of girl.' uttered the Major, stifling a giggle.

'Hoghorn.'

The Major peeped through a gap between the neatly stacked logs and could indeed see Hoghorn gliding purposely up the lane towards the cottage. They edged their way around the wood pile for a better view and caught sight of Smallpott welcoming her inside.

'You don't suppose he's shagging her do you?' said Henderson. The two of them managed to resist laughing out loud.

'He's got more chance of parting the Red Sea.'

'Moses Smallpott,' added Henderson in a barely stifled high pitch voice and added 'Chastity, it's not her name . . . it's an instruction.' He was on a roll.

'I've pissed myself.'

'Me too.'

'Why do you think Hoghorn was paying a visit to Smallpott then?' asked Henderson as the two of them were setting about cleaning up the brewery the following evening.

'I don't know, it doesn't make any sense, she's well catered for whatever the outcome, she has no need to sucker up to the likes of Smallpott.' The Major was genuinely puzzled.

After a pause, Henderson asked 'Is there a chance you could produce an heir, I know a couple of women who'd agree to you know . . . help out.' offered Henderson.

'Not a hope I'm afraid old chap, it's a long story, suffice to say that an old army injury put paid the reproductive department, the gun still works but the shells are empty.' he didn't want Henderson the think he was less of a man.

'Pity, what about in the past?' Henderson enquired knowing they were sufficiently close enough that this sort of personal question wouldn't be out of place for a friend to ask.

'Oh if only - trouble is, wild oats are sown wildly amongst other oats and come harvest time no one knows who planted what where.'

Over the next couple of weeks, they managed to convert the boiler into a still and had collected together over three hundred bottles of Paraffin Percy's wine from some very willing contributors. Henderson had transported these in a wheelbarrow under a covering of compost, right under the nose of Hoghorn who viewed everything with suspicion. The

Major had concluded to himself that if Hoghorn had to choose sides in the future of the estate, it wouldn't be his. In fact, she was probably reporting to Makepeace and even more ominously, Smallpott.

Henderson had sorted the bottles out and divided them into groups, light, dark and cloudy. Using small samples blended together and tested in the still up Jacks Bottom, they worked out which were the best combinations and which were better for just cleaning the pipes.

At the same time, Clifford at the Stonely Arms Inn had resurrected the old hidden pipe work under the bar to the harmless-looking spare tap above the sink. In the cellar, a cupboard and some hasty plastering, hid the reconnected vital link.

Between them, they had worked out that they could supply the pub for about a year at best, with the limited stock. It was to turn out that they had seriously underestimated its popularity.

Clifford, a man of great resources, found that he could add "Special Brew" to both spirits and beer. It certainly improved the taste of the beer and the small surcharge for 'topping up', as it became known, was accepted happily, mainly because one pint was the alcoholic equivalent of two.

It was, with good fortune, that Henderson had cause to visit old Percy's farm one evening, now run by his son and daughter. When the conversation turned to the subject of Percy himself, Denis Henderson asked casually if they had any of their fathers wine left and to his astonishment they said yes. They told him to take a look under the kitchen table they were sat at.

Henderson lifted up the edge of the tablecloth to reveal that it was supported on four large barrels, 144 gallons in fact.

'There's another barrel in the barn but we use that for tupping.'

'You force-feed the ram before mating it with the ewes?' asked Henderson, somewhat taken aback.

'Good God no, he'd never make it that far, we paint it on his balls so we can see who he's mated with, the wine's blue and it stains.' they laughed.

That evening, Henderson walked back to his room over the old stable block to work out how much wood he would need to make four table legs.

That was nearly five years ago now.

The Major, having finished his breakfast, retired to the study upstairs, he had some serious thinking to do and patently aware that he only had a month left at the Hall. The past five years had passed quickly. If he were honest with himself, he had become far more comfortable than he had realised, the Hall had enveloped him completely to the extent that it actually felt like home and he would be sorry to see it go and even sorrier that Smallpott would be getting his grubby hands on it.

He had, after the reading of his mothers last and apparently only will, consulted his friend at his London club as to its validity and he was bluntly honest. Despite its unusual content, it was correctly drafted and executed, the meaning of the will was clear and concise. His only hope was to contest it at the last moment but even then, it would probably be a lost cause, cost him a fortune and would only delay the inevitable. It was just a way of buying time in the most expensive way.

Something that hurt more, was the embarrassment of what might be seen as social demotion, his title remained, of course, intact but a Duke living in a gatehouse cottage, a servants abode, at the very entrance of the estate that he should be living in and having Smallpott lording over it over one and all left a bitter taste.

He had had a couple of meetings with Makepeace who was sympathetic but unmovable and the only thing that had been resolved was being allowed to keep his fathers few personal possessions discovered in a trunk in the cellar. It sadly didn't include the Bentley which was deemed part of the estate.

It was with this thought, he retrieved his father's diaries from their secret hiding-place with a mind to destroying them. He had flipped through them briefly before and knew they showed the demise of the brewery through what was plainly bad local economics.

His train of thought was interrupted by the sound of a bicycle coming up the gravel drive. The Major was expecting a letter. Pre-empting a visit by Hoghorn, he placed the diaries on the far corner of the desk with their spines clearly in view of anyone approaching. The Major wasn't sure why he did this, he was perhaps curious to see if she reacted in anyway.

On cue, Hoghorn entered the study in her usual noiseless fashion which still continued to irk him.

'A letter has arrived for you.' she said, stating the obvious and placing it down before him. He picked it up and sliced it open with the silver letter opener whilst looking at her throat.

'Anything else?' asked the Major, he knew she was interested in this letter, it had a wax seal on the back which prevented it being steamed open, he also knew it was from his London contact at the club.

'Are you in for lunch?' she asked, stopping pointedly short of a 'Sir'.

'Not today Hoghorn, thank you.'

With that, she turned and left the room. She'd seen the books alright and they had had an effect unnoticeable unless you were looking for it. She had subconsciously reached up to her high-buttoned neck, as if touching a concealed crucifix.

He didn't know if she wore one, as she was always prudishly-dressed in what can only be described as a neck-to-floor, Victorian style - she was a woman misplaced in time. It had been a point of amusement to many, that corsets and bodices actually enhanced the female figure, giving it a defined form from a period where sex was more than a dirty word and performed with windows, curtains and eyes closed. He had never paid attention to her as a woman before, after all, she had been his nanny and a servant. A thought flashed passed him, had she been a wet nurse nanny? The idea of him feeding off her teat made him feel uneasy. That was beside the point, she had reacted.

The letter appeared to be from his contact in London. Major Stonely had gone to the city last month to make some financial arrangements, transferring his 'special pension fund' in India back to his account in England. It would prove to be a valuable lifeline, now his time at the Hall was drawing to a close.

His stay at the club had been a pleasant one. It was delightfully civil and quiet. A place where no questions were asked and no answers expected, it was also the only place where he used his title, in preference to Major.

He had arranged to meet Walton St-John for lunch in a private dining room at the club. They had been friends in his early army career and kept in touch and occasionally swapped favours. The Major had always trusted his advice and he had useful contacts within the city.

They had inevitably wandered on to the subject of the Majors inheritance. Walton had the ability to look at things simply, by brushing aside unnecessary complications and creating an uncluttered, clearer picture. He reminded the Major of his original thoughts of discrediting Smallpott.

'Lets be honest, you're not really in a position to do this yourself. First of all, time is against you and secondly, you'd be rubbish at it.'

The Major laughed, it was true, too much of shutting the stable door after the horse had bolted and he wouldn't know where to start. After all, he had spent much of his career covering things up.

'Any last-minute suggestions?'

'William Roystone, he's a sort of private detective chappie, discrete, experienced, expensive and select. You put your case forward and if it interests him, he lets you know.'

'And does he get results?'

'Oh yes, not what I wanted to get but I paid for the truth and got it.'

'I'd like to meet him, perhaps dinner this week?'

'He only deals through the post, no contact, PO Box number only.'

Later that evening, the Major had written out the details of the situation, being as honest as he dare, Walton warned him that Royston wanted only facts, not thoughts and to enclose a cheque for five hundred pounds. It was non-returnable.

The Major unfolded the letter, it was blank but inside was a printed business card, it said simply: William Roystone, at your service.

Chapter 8: Timothy arrives in the village

Timothy Montague drew up outside the Stonely Arms, in the battered Morris Eight that had been assigned to him by the department. It was all part of the cover story, they had told him. This was to be his first and probably last covert operation as an investigator for His Majesties Customs and Excise, although he didn't know that.

'Think of it as being a sort of spy.' Mr. Mackenzie, the department supervisor had said.

'Do I get a gun?' asked Timothy.

'Almost, you get this.' and was handed a book on bird watching.

Timothy was struck by the village inn. The building was like an illustration out of some old history book. A magnificent 16th century timber-framed coaching inn. The black beams stood in stark contrast to the white mortar infill and not a straight line was to be seen. Each leaded window was slightly askew, the parallels weren't parallel and the thatched roof undulated like a slow ripple on a still pond. It was a far cry from the utilitarian brick office back at work.

Up until this moment, he had thought of this as some grand adventure and an opportunity to prove himself. However the time had come to take that step forward and present himself as Timothy Montague bird watcher and spy.

'Morning! Timothy Montague bird watcher,' said Timothy reaching out his hand. 'Do you have a room for rent, landlord?' . . . 'Lovely establishment you have here,' . . . 'Possibly one or two weeks, I should imagine.'

Jack Thompson, the village butcher across the square, watched fascinated as the young man sat alone in the car gesticulating with one hand and shaking an imaginary one with the other. He appeared to be addressing the steering wheel. Thompson continued to scrape his butchers block slowly, mouth slightly open and wishing he could lip read like Ma Gibbons when she had caught him out calling her a deaf, wrinkled old witch.

Timothy rehearsed his entrance for another minute but it still failed to sound natural. He knew he was just delaying the inevitable.

He'd never been a very social creature, naturally timid and totally inept with strangers, just fumbling and bumbling his way along. Work colleagues were somehow different, expectations were initially low and he was always the 'New boy' so to speak, slowly working his way to familiarity.

It had taken a couple of months before he had felt confident enough to join his colleagues in the local pub for a Friday afternoon pint. He would certainly have never gone in alone. Now he faced his greatest challenge yet, acting.

Timothy got out of the car, gathered up his things and headed towards the inns nail-studded, oak door. Grasping the iron handle, he entered the dimly-lit interior in what he perceived as a meaningful manner. He just caught sight of a sign above his head that said 'Please Mind your . . .' His brain had assumed 'Step,' the reality was 'Head.'

A few minutes later, he opened his eyes to find himself sat on a chair in a corner of the bar. A pair of breasts were swinging in front of him in a very low-cut top.

'Hello, that must have hurt!' said the breasts, or rather the smiling young lady they were attached to.

'Ah.' was the best he could manage at that moment. He realised she was holding a damp cloth to his forehead and had her other hand resting on his knee, supporting her weight.

'I think that will do now, Shirley,' said a man who slowly came into focus as the breasts disappeared; he had the persona of the landlord. 'Name's Clifford, I'm the landlord - you can call me Cliff.' said Clifford.

'Ah.' said Timothy, who had yet to utter a proper word since he had entered.

'You missed the sign then? Hard as oak, those beams, because they are - no damage done.'

There was a distant snigger from the shadows at the other end of the room.

'Timothy Montague.' said Timothy, extending a hand.

'You selling something?' asked Clifford.

'No, just looking for a place to stay.'

'That's alright then.' Clifford smiled, took his hand and yanked him upright. Timothy's brain protested at this sudden moment by sending a stabbing pain to the back of his eyes.

'Fiver a week in advance, all in.'

'Splendid.' replied Timothy, realising his intention of being in control from the moment he entered, had evaded him. He threw his prepared mental script away; the landlord and he were on different pages.

'What'll you have to drink then Tim? On the house, make up for that bang on the noggin.'

Timothy looked along the bar, there was just the one hand pump. He wisely decided to keep his head still, mouth closed and pointed to it.

'Poachers Pig, popular choice that,' grinned Clifford. He glanced over to the shadows and back again.

'You here on business then?'

'Oh no, purely pleasure, I'm a bird watcher, it's my hobby.'

'Oh yes?' replied the landlord cocking his head to one side.

'Feathered.' added Timothy, catching on to the implication amazingly quickly.

The breasts known as Shirley had reappeared with a foaming pint and offered it up. Timothy took it carefully and tried to saunter over to the bar, where he placed one elbow down in a nonchalant manner, into the ashtray.

'Yes, I'm keen to get into the countryside and study our feathered friends.' said Timothy, by way of conversation.

'Have you seen the great tit around here yet?' asked a voice from the shadows.

'Not as yet.' he replied.

'Pity, we've all seen one this morning.' This was accompanied by muted laughter. That one metaphorically flew over Timothy's head. He took a sip of his pint and was a little surprised that it actually had a hint of bacon.

'Interesting ale, Landlord.' said Timothy.

'Got some Cow Pat Porter coming Wednesday.' replied Clifford.

Timothy was starting to feel a little uncomfortable. He had been the centre of attention for far too long and felt a need to get away and collect his thoughts, but just getting away would be good. He took another gulp of his beer, pulled out his wallet and extracted a five pound note for the landlord.

As if on cue, Shirley asked Clifford which room to give him. It was decided the Chatterley suite was the most suitable. There was more muted laughter from the shadows.

Timothy downed his pint hastily and followed Shirley up the stairs at the back of the inn. She had insisted on carrying his cases and leading the way. Her skirt was, in Timothy's mind, very short and he glimpsed what he thought might be a stocking-top. He politely averted his eyes going up. He also noted every wooden step creaked. At the top, she turned right and headed down the short hall, stopping at a door at the end marked 'Chatterley', it was carved neatly into the wood. He followed her inside.

'Would you like it on the bed?' she asked.

Timothy opened his mouth but nothing came out.

'Your case.' She added, smiling.

'Oh yes, thank you.' he managed to answer, turning red.

As the door closed behind her, he instantly deflated in relief. He took off his jacket and sat on the edge of the bed. What had he let himself in for, he thought? His entrance had been a total failure and wondered if he could really keep up this pretence, and as for Shirley, he couldn't keep his mind off her. He had never been so close to so much free-flowing flesh before and had a strong stirring in his loins. He hoped she hadn't noticed.

The Chatterley suite was at the front of the inn. In reality, it was a single room with a bath behind a curtain. There was a small writing desk in front of the window, a brass bedstead in the centre and a dark oak wardrobe next to the door. It was one of those that creaked ominously when it opened, which it did every time you passed. The ceiling had those familiar black beams that featured prominently within the building but fortunately, well above his head this time. The wallpaper had a chintzy rose pattern that gave the room a slight feminine feel.

Timothy stood up and went over to the window. Through the net curtain, he had a clear view of the village square and surrounding buildings. He decided to change and go for a little walk around to acquaint himself with the surroundings. He turned around, unbuttoned his fly and let his trousers drop to the floor.

It was at that moment, the door opened and Shirley stepped into the room, 'Forgot your towels.' Timothy, in an instant, lifted up the lid of his suitcase on the bed to block her view of his near-nakedness and semi-erection.

'I'll pop them in the bathroom, shall I?' It was one of those questions that didn't require an answer but Timothy nodded anyway. She bent down and placed them on a chair next to the bath, confirming his earlier suspicions of stocking tops. It didn't help his awkward situation.

'If you need help with anything?' she said, looking at the suitcase and back to Timothy 'Just ask. I'm very good with my hands.' As she left, she reached out and closed the wardrobe door that had swung open, the one with the mirror on. Timothy was completely oblivious of what she might have caught sight of in its reflection.

'What do you make of him then Shirley?' asked Clifford as she came back down to the bar.

'He's a bit stiff after his long drive,' they all laughed. 'I don't think you've got much to worry about, he's not exactly brimming with intelligence.'

'Not a clue?' asked Clifford.

'Not a clue.' replied Shirley.

Timothy, whose embarrassing problem having slowly subsided, changed after having now locked the door. He sat on the edge of the bed and was sorting out his suitcase. In order to keep up the pretence, the department had supplied an expense account, allowing him to purchase anything he thought necessary to retain his cover. Three second-hand books on British birds he thought essential. One small one to carry about, one for the bedside stand and one, he had left in the car in clear view. He also had a pair of binoculars, camera, notepad, several pencils, a pair of stout walking shoes, socks, plus fours, deer stalker hat, plastic raincoat, rucksack and sandwich tin. In the back of the car, he had left a one man tent, a billycan for water, matches, torch and an Ordinance Survey map of the area.

He had to admit that a bird watcher disguise was a master stroke; it allowed him to wander around legitimately in pursuit of his fictitious hobby.

He reached into the case and pulled out a package wrapped in brown paper and string. It was heavy for its size and had an oily, metallic smell about it. It used to be his fathers, apparently.

Timothy had been born - much to the surprise of his mother Ellen who had taken every precaution against it - in a tiny cottage in an equally tiny village on the south coast. He never knew his father but come to that, neither did his mother.

She had always told him that it was a romance with an officer in the army, but he'd been sent on a 'special mission' and been killed in a skirmish abroad. He had the impression it was somewhere in Italy - she always went a little glassy eyed whenever that country was mentioned.

The reality was quite different. Ellen had a certain charm about her that endeared her to soldiers, but not the ordinary soldiers, junior officers - she did have certain standards. She was often their first sexual encounter and regarded herself as a sort of training ground for the inexperienced upper ranks. It was a service she gave all too freely.

When Ellen fell pregnant, there was understandable panic amongst the young officers. She had seen some heavy military action so-to-speak, but she didn't want sympathy, or a husband come to that. The officers, gentlemen to the last, did the honourable thing and a financial agreement was reached between themselves. Every month, each would deposit one pound into her post office account to support the child and keep her silence. It might not have seemed much of a gesture but fifty three pounds a month came in jolly useful. She had, after all, known a lot of good men. She viewed this as a sort of military widow's pension without actually being married, or a widow.

Timothy grew up oblivious of this arrangement. A timid boy, tall, gangly and perhaps a little slow but well meaning and polite. Strings had been pulled with her 'officer friends' in later life and job opportunities became available for young Timmy. Sadly, these were often short-lived. It hadn't been through want of trying, Timothy was eager to please, he just didn't fit in, he was a bit of a dreamer.

Now he was working for the Customs and Excise department. Again, some slight pressure had been brought to bear and the position of junior office assistant had conveniently manifested itself. He was, in essence, a glorified tea boy, runner and filing clerk. For two years, he pottered about with his rather mundane tasks whilst being enthralled listening to stories of captured smugglers, clandestine meetings and infiltration of gangs of organised crime. He dreamed of being part of the investigation team, he wanted a taste of adventure - he was Bulldog Drummond and Sherlock Holmes rolled into one just without the opportunity, knowledge or unfortunately the intelligence that goes with it.

Mackenzie, the supervisor, had laughed when Timothy asked if it were possible to be transferred to the investigation department. He was well aware his presence in the department was the result of some favour further up the chain and Timothy was a burden he had to bear.

It was one evening when Mackenzie was having a drink with the head of investigations, that a plan was conceived. If Timothy were to be transferred and it was seen as some sort of promotion, it opened a one way door. Timothy would be sent on a very minor mission as a test of his natural abilities before formal training began. He would fail of course, and the doors firmly closed behind him - problem solved. The head of Investigations just happened to be Mackenzie's brother.

Timothy was beside himself when Mackenzie summoned him to his office and told him that he was to be transferred to the investigation branch and would be sent on a mission in a purely observational capacity, as a test.

The mission chosen was to investigate the claim of an illegal brewery set up in a country village. The claim was a genuine one, as was the destination but it warranted little interest and was more-or-less-likely based on some minor revenge scheme by a crossed neighbour or friend who had been diddled out of their share of some local home-brew.

Any investigator would deduce this within a couple of days and that would be the end of the case but planting a seed of exaggeration in Timothy's mind would be enough to blow it out of proportion.

Back at the inn and having attired himself in his bird watching garb, he descended the creaking wooden stairs to the bar below. No one seemed to pay him much attention as he left the pub and turned right. His aim was to get some sort of idea of the layout of the land.

The inn was at the top of the village square. Immediately ahead of him was the entrance to Stonely Hall but to its left was a narrow tree lined lane.

He strode off in that direction, allowing him to quickly get out of sight of anyone watching.

He knew a little about beer brewing, he had been on a visit to a local brewery to act as an assistant once, when measures were being checked. It was one of the few exciting times he'd had. He reasoned with himself that a potential brewery was unlikely to be in the village itself but hidden away from prying eyes. It would need a water supply, have a fire and access for transportation. The surrounding farmland and wooded areas would be ideally suited.

About a mile later, Timothy reached the end of the lane, it petered out into little more than a footpath. The surrounding land was either ploughed, or had cattle. The few buildings that were visible, were little more than open barns used to store hay and equipment.

He checked his map. The village of Stonely wasn't well defined. The dominant features were the two hills to the north, the taller had the word '(ruin)' on the top. The surrounding area was given to woodland or open pasture. The Stonely Estate, although large, just didn't feature at all, other than a small black square that could be mistaken for a farm. The nearest major road bypassed the area completely and went on to another much larger village to the east called Stoneleigh, this was where Timothy Montague should have been, but he didn't know that.

He started the walk back to the village. After about a quarter of a mile, he felt the urge to relieve himself. The lane had bushy hedgerows along each side and checking all was clear, he stepped off the path and unbuttoned his flies, relaxed and stared into the middle distance.

'Supper's at 7 o'clock, Mr. Montague.' called out Shirley, as she cycled past down the lane. 'Don't forget to shake.'

Timothy stood motionless and glowed red. The only sound was that of urine splattering off his walking boots.

He returned a couple of hours later, having followed another small path that was truly overgrown but again yielded no results.

As he entered the inn, once more it fell silent. He remembered to duck this time and the gentle murmur of voices recommenced. He had a feeling they were a little disappointed.

Back in his room, he sat down on the bed and put his head in his hands and wished he could start again. He just seemed to be making a fool of himself, and as for Shirley; she just seemed to pop up whenever he had his trousers down.

He spent the last of the afternoon studying the map for likely vantage points and brushing up on his bird watching knowledge, just in case. At six thirty, he decided to show his face downstairs, realising it would look odd if he didn't and he was unsure of the dining arrangements. He freshened himself up in the bathroom and left the room, locking the door behind him as always. At the foot of the creaking stairs, he noticed a door that was usually shut, was now wide open and a wonderful smell wafted out, it was roast lamb. He poked his head around the door and discovered the dining room, it was small but welcoming.

Timothy sat down at the smallest table just under the window. There were four other men sat in the room, all of whom looked like locals, they paused for a moment when he entered but carried on talking once they saw who it was. It was almost a sense of relief he felt. He was worrying too much.

Shirley appeared out of a door at the far end and walked over to Timothy.

'Mr. Montague' she smiled, 'We have lamb chops with veg or a steak and kidney pie with beer gravy. What do you fancy?'

Timothy was sure she pushed her breasts out further than necessary when she said 'What do you fancy'.

'The lamb will be fine.' he stuttered.

'And a pint, perhaps?' she smiled.

'Yes, a pint, thank you.' he replied, instantly regretting it - he'd forgotten the bacon after-taste that came with it. Shirley walked off with an enthusiastic wiggle that poor old Timothy could hardly take his eyes off.

After the meal, he sat back looking at his pocket book of birds, while he finished his pint. Best not to rush off too quickly, he thought, try to meld in sort of thing, blend, yes, catch some drifting conversation whilst pretending not to hear. He thought of moving into the bar but that would mean another pint.

Shirley came over to clear his plate.

'Was everything alright, Mr. Montague?' She asked.

'Oh yes,' he paused, 'I don't mind if you call me Timothy.'

'Ok Timothy' she said and leaned forward, bringing her bosom clearly into view.

'Would you like a bit more?'

'Yes please.' he answered and went bright red when he realised she meant another pint - as her hand was resting on his empty glass. He lifted his book up to head-height to cover his glowing face. Hopefully, with the light of the window behind him, it wasn't too obvious.

That wasn't his only problem. He was sporting another erection, he couldn't move even if he wanted to. Timothy was totally inexperienced when it came to the female gender. He had never seen a naked woman before, the closest he'd come was a statue in his local museum, pure white alabaster with a magnificent bottom, he couldn't understand his attraction to it. Sex was also a mystery to him, he knew that some sort of physical contact was involved and he had a rough idea, he'd seen dogs in the park, but it seemed too ridiculous to be true. He regarded the spontaneous erections as his 'affliction.'

Timothy took his fresh pint and retired to his room for the rest of the evening. Tomorrow he would start exploring more thoroughly.

Chapter 9: Over the Hill

7 o'clock the next morning and there was a loud tap on the door of the Chatterley suite. 'Breakfast is ready.' called out Clifford, the landlord, in a cheery voice. Timothy was already up and dressed. He'd woken at five that morning having slept reasonably well, despite being in a strange bed with its well worn body-shaped hollow in the centre. He had passed the time watching the village gently easing into life, whilst browsing through his bird-spotting books. It was in stark contrast to the hurried pace of town life that he had become accustomed to. Here, people stopped and chatted in the square below and women gathered in the bakers shop for their daily bread and gossip.

Breakfast was a very crowded plate of sausages, eggs, bacon, black pudding and fried bread, set in a glistening puddle of what was possibly lard. It was clear this hadn't been prepared by Shirley and was a far cry from his normal boiled egg and soldiers at home.

Outside, the sun was shining brightly and casting early shadows on the ground, birds were in song and the air was a little on the sharp side. Today, Timothy had decided to set off south through the village.

Stonely village had once been mentioned in the doomsday book, 'One cow' was its singular claim to fame after that it had remained comfortably quiet. The main feature, was the square itself. An ornate, bronze, but noticeably-dry fountain stood in the centre. The scalloped basin had long since been given over to a well tended flowerbed. The central figure was that of Bacchus, the god of wine standing proudly, holding aloft a bunch of grapes. Timothy noted that it was both naked and incredibly well-endowed. This feature was accentuated by its smooth, polished surface which also extended to its buttocks whilst the rest of the casting remained tinted with the green patina of time. Momentarily, he wondered where the water had come out; he hoped it was from the cup held in its other hand!

The inn itself, was perhaps the most dominate building in the square. Bright in its whiteness against the lush green trees behind. The rest of the village square had naturally evolved around it, a trend made popular in the middle ages.

Most of the buildings seemed to be late 17th to mid 18th century, some still had the wooden framework visible, whilst others had been covered up with a mortar skin or refaced in locally made mismatched brick. Idyllic would have been a good word, picturesque another.

Directly opposite the inn was Thompson's butchers shop, it was quite narrow but then passing trade wasn't his custom, he was very much a service rather than a retailer. This was the overall impression that was slowly dawning in Timothy's mind, it was as if the village could carry on functioning even if the rest of the country sunk into the sea, and if it had, they'd just open up a fish mongers. It seemed to be totally self-reliant and grateful for it.

Next door to the butchers was the baker and combined tea room. It was called rather unimaginatively, Bakers & Tea Room. The waft of freshly-baked bread was unmistakable in the morning air and drew custom like a magnet. Through the large windows, he could see the small tables with their neatly ironed, chequered table cloths adorned with an array of condiments, carefully placed in size order. It would be a popular place for the ladies of the village to gather socially, they certainly didn't frequent the inn, that was for sure.

Almost leaning against this, was the post office and village store, it also appeared to double as the chemist as well. A poster in the window advertised the qualities of sunlight soap in gaudy yellow. It was closed.

At the southern end of the square, stood the ironmongers whose shop front spilled over into the square with a cluttered array of knick-knacks and whatnots. There were things with spouts, spokes, straps and springs that wouldn't be out of place in a museum or medieval torture chamber.

The rest of the buildings were, thankfully, simple thatched cottages with one or two displayed crude hand-made signs outside. Dr Strange apparently lived next door to Mr.Todd the barber and undertaker. An unsettling pairing in many respects, Timothy thought.

As the square tapered away, the tree-lined lane continued gracefully south. It was dotted here and there with the odd cottage along the way until they eventually petered out, giving way to farmland glimpsed occasionally through the high hedgerows.

Clifford and George, his cellar man, watched Timothy disappear around the slight curve in the road and into the distance.

'You know, I just can't make up my mind about that young man, something just doesn't sit properly. I think Shirley's right, he's a bottle short of a crate but we can't afford to have him stumbling about too much can we?' George just nodded; country folk can say so much with so little. 'He's going to have a good day today though.' Clifford added.

It had been purely by chance that Timothy stumbled upon the village at all, even though it was the wrong one. Local sign posts were scant or non-existent. Many had of course, been removed during the war and melted down for munitions as well as to hamper any invading forces who would presumably spend the rest of the war lost in country lanes living off blackberries.

What Timothy was looking for, was a hill, not normally too much of a problem in the countryside but his sights were set on the highest and that was clearly behind the Stonely estate. Yesterday's brief exploration had revealed nothing other than farmland and dense woods. There had been no hint of a path up to the hill itself. Trying to sneak through the estate or even skirting around the edge was out of the question, it would risk bringing attention to himself and so his only option now was to try to find a way around the back.

After about half a mile down the lane and well out of sight of the village, he came across a stile tucked deep into the hedgerow. A path could be seen curving off in the rough direction of the hill. It was clear it was used but not frequently.

The first leg of the journey had been easy, a gentle slope upwards, passing the ruins of an old abandoned farmhouse now little more than stumpy walls tracing the outline of what was once someone's home. A little further on brought him to a shaded wood. The tree branches up high forming a tight, almost lightproof, canopy. The ground bore witness to the power of sunlight, or rather the lack of it. Only moss and lichen existed down here and it emanated a rich, almost sweet, composting odour.

At the far edge of the wood, the path had become almost indistinguishable, a clear sign that this was as far as anyone went. Timothy fought on against bramble, nettle and gorse. Thorns tore at his long socks and plus four walking trousers. In the densest of foliage, he found himself almost wading through with his arms well above his head.

The semicircular route did indeed lead up to the top of the hill. It had taken Timothy almost two hours to reach just below the summit but was rewarded with a spectacular view of the surrounding countryside. Timothy drank it in.

It was nearly 11 o'clock and he had expended so much energy that he was looking forward to an early lunch. Settling down, he opened up his rucksack and pulled out the cloth-wrapped bundle on top. Clifford, the landlord, on discovering Timothy was going to be out for lunch, had prepared a packed lunch for him, 'All part of the service.' Clifford had said, well insisted, really.

Inside was what he thought was going to be a couple of rounds of sandwiches, instead it was just the one. One large three inch thick sandwich stuffed with rare cooked beef, horseradish source, tomato and lettuce. It didn't fit in his mouth. Things were so very different in the country, rationing was still on but it seemed to have no effect here and Timothy was very happy about that.

Clifford had also supplied a bottle of beer to go with his lunch and he had no choice in this matter as he had substituted it for his normal water can. Ever thoughtful, there was a bottle-opener tied to the neck with string.

Having managed to eat his lunch by tearing chunks off and washing them down with sips of beer that, for once, didn't taste of bacon, he set about drawing a rough sketch of the patchwork landscape before him. Isolated farm buildings and barns littered the area, small ponds were dotted here and there. He noted that grazing pastures seemed to favour closeness to the village, whereas arable land was generally more distance. He also had, for the first time, a clear view of the Stonely estate.

The main building, which he had heard referred to as the Hall, stood in a large horseshoe-shaped plot of land covering several acres, not that Timothy had any concept of how large an acre was. It was surrounded almost completely by trees of many varieties, noticeable by their different colours and forms. The far side merged into the dense woodland he had tried to penetrate yesterday. From his vantage point, he could just make out a small cottage in a clearing. He made a mental note to investigate that more thoroughly. In what Timothy would have called the back garden and some distance from the hall, was a lake emerging from the trees. It was probably ornamental rather than natural and surrounded almost entirely with bulrushes, with the exception what looked like a boathouse tucked away in the tree line. There was also a small island in the middle. Using his binoculars, he saw that the islands centre-piece was a fountain, the twin of Bacchus he had seen earlier in the village square. It had always confused Timothy that fountains, based on the male human form, spouted water from every orifice or grasped container except the most obvious natural one.

From this high vantage point, Timothy was getting a better feel for the lay of the land. The immediate landscape was that of a valley, shallow at first, with the lane and the village rising to a slight plateau where the Stonely Hall estate nestled comfortably. It then rose to form the two hills behind where he was now sat. Shirley's cleavage came to mind.

Timothy belched loudly. There was an odd aftertaste of beetroot. Next, he had to put some entries in his bird watching notebook which he planned to leave in the bar or dining room accidentally, he was sure someone would take a peek. Binoculars at the ready, he watched the landscape before him for birds, people and just maybe the tell-tale signs of steam or smoke from a hidden brewery. He had already dismissed the inn because it was, of course, too obvious and he'd have smelt the distinct floral nature of the hops boiling.

It was well over two hours later when Timothy woke up. Disorientated for a while, his situation slowly came in to focus; he'd never done that before. He raised himself up on his elbows and looked at the beer bottle; it hadn't seemed that strong. It must have been the climb up the hill that had weakened his reserve, apart from that, he was dying for a wee.

He reassessed his surroundings. He had a clear and unrestricted view of the surrounding area and consequently those in the village likewise. The tree line was a good quarter of the way down from his position; this of course left him in full view and he needed to pee quite badly now.

A brainwave lumbered its way in. he would dig a small hole beside him, roll over onto it, unbutton his fly and relieve himself whilst holding a book in front of his face with his other hand. It would look like he was just lying on his stomach reading, perfect and there was no risk of Shirley catching him unawares, especially up here. He was safe.

Back at the Stonely Arms, Clifford stood at an upstairs window with an old telescope looking up at the distant hill.

'I think he's having it off with a rabbit hole.'

'Aww, let me see.' said Shirley almost snatching it out of Clifford's grasp.

'You seem very interested in him, girl.'

'He's sweet.'

'He's stupid, he's even got a book on how to stick your tadger down a rabbit hole.'

'Probably something to do with that bottle of beer you gave him I shouldn't wonder, bless him.'

'Just slowing him down.' grinned Clifford.

Suitably relieved, Timothy packed up his now considerably lighter rucksack and thought about starting back down towards the village. It had taken a couple of hours to get up there, going down would be easier but he didn't relish the idea of those brambles and thorns again. Logic wasn't normally timothy's strong point but he knew a straight line was the shortest route and was sure he could, with caution, weave his way down through the fields almost directly to the village.

Getting to the bottom of the hill had been easy, momentum helped him on his way but the closer to the bottom he came, the denser the plant life. Eventually, he broke out of the foliage and entered the first of many fields. It was now, he realised that at ground level, he had lost sight of the village because of trees and tall hedgerows. He wished he'd paid more attention in the scouts now. He surmised that keeping the hill behind him, he would eventually come across the lane. He had, until then, been quite confident but the further he went, the softer the ground seemed to become. Underfoot was starting to become decidedly squishy. By half past five, he was up to his knees in it and trying to work out if he was over half way, with the tentative thought of going back.

'Evening Timmy.' came a voice off to his right. Timothy recognised a local who had been at breakfast that morning. He was leaning on a small wooden gate in the hedge watching him.

'Evening.' replied Timothy.

'Good spot for the Marsh Warbler, that.'

'Yes, just what I was thinking.' replied Timothy - he wasn't. The farmer smiled back at him and raised a beer glass to his mouth. It was now that Timothy realised where he was, right beside the back of the inn. A warming sense of relief flooded over him. After trudging his way across the rest of the field he entered through the gate and into the back garden, sat down on a bench and took off his shoes and socks and let the marshy water dribble out. The farmer was sat over the other side smoking a pipe and paid him no further attention. Suitably drained, in so many senses of the word, he entered by the back door. In the back lobby he could hear the general hubbub from the bar beyond but managed to get up to his room unseen. No one was any the wiser, except everyone was, of course.

Locking the door behind him and making sure Shirley wasn't in the wardrobe, he took off his wet trousers and draped them over the end of the bed with his socks. A bath would be a good idea and drew back the curtain that separated the bedroom from the bathroom. He looked at the bath for quite a while. It was half full of hot water and fresh towels were neatly folded up on the toilet seat with a new bar of Sunlight soap on top.

It was uncanny how everyone seemed to know where he was and what he was doing all the time, however the hot bath was enticing and a welcome relief.

Suitably refreshed and with just a towel over him, he laid on the bed to contemplate his next move. There was a knock at the door.

'Just a minute Shirley.' called out Timothy.

'How'd you know it was me?' she answered through the door.

'Just a guess.'

Timothy slipped on his dressing gown and opened the door slightly. Shirley stood there, as vivacious as ever. In her hand was a tray with a bowl of soup and buttered rolls.

'I've brought you something to nibble on.' she said with her cheeky smile. Timothy found himself looking at her breasts which seemed to be fighting for attention. Coming quickly to his senses, he opened the door. She stepped inside and immediately spotted his wet clothing hanging from the end of the bed.

'Would you like me to wash those for you?' she asked, handing him the tray. 'It's no trouble.'

'Oh that's very kind of you, thank you Shirley.'

'I hope you didn't mind me running the bath, it's just that the old boiler in the cellar was working well, so I took advantage of the extra hot water, I thought you might like to slip into something warm when you got back.' Timothy felt himself starting to blush and the front of his dressing gown had begun to twitch.

'Is it just birds your interested in?' she asked as she folded up the damp trousers.

'Yes.' replied Timothy who hadn't moved from the spot. Both his hands were tied up holding the tray and his problem was growing at an alarming rate, threatening to fight its way out of the overlap of his dressing gown. He leaned forward slightly, hoping it might become less obvious. Shirley hadn't noticed.

'No interest in rabbits then?'

'No, not really, why do you ask?' he replied a little perplexed and regretted the question instantly as it increased the time he had to stand there.

'Oh, no reason, just wondered.'

It was only now, that Timothy thought of lowering the tray down to waist level and covering his growing embarrassment.

Shirley bent down to pick up Timothy's damp socks and he couldn't resist glancing at her gravity-defying breasts, that by rights, should have fallen out. His erection had now escaped its confines and stood in its full glory tapping the underneath of the tray causing small ripples to form in the soup bowl.

Shirley draped his damp clothes over her arm and started to leave. Sensing something wasn't quite right with Timothy, she asked, 'Is something up - would you like me to put the tray on the table for you?'

'No, I'm fine thank you' there was a slight hint of panic in his voice and his grip on the tray tightened. A smile crossed her face as it dawned on her what the problem could be.

'Well you know where I am if you need anything.' She said as she left the room.

The moment the door closed, Timothy disgraced himself.

Chapter 10: Be still!

Timothy had spent the last two days exploring the surrounding countryside in ever increasing circles. His travels had revealed the beauty of rolling hills and babbling brooks. A landscape littered with ruins of old flint barns and isolated Shepard's huts. Bountiful hedgerows of nature's fruits were laid before him, ripe for the picking, which he did often. He'd even fashioned a tall walking stick from a broken branch. Timothy was starting to meld into country life and he'd have an accent soon if he wasn't careful.

It was time for a change of tack. If there was a brewery here, he was looking in the wrong place for the wrong thing. Given plenty of time to think, he had come to the conclusion he had set his sights too broadly. There was no brewery in the sense he was used to, no production line, no bottling plant, no transport system and certainly no five o'clock whistle. This was the countryside and country ways were different. Here, there was a mend and make-do attitude, an unhurriedness in a - it's ready when it's ready - sort of way. If a brewery existed here, it was probably right under his nose in plain sight.

This morning, he was going to investigate the woods he had discovered on his first day. He knew the lane opposite the inn was a dead end and there were no clear paths into the wood itself. However, from the higher vantage point of the hill he had climbed the other day, he had spotted the cottage tucked away within. He had made a mental note at the time to investigate and now was that time.

Bidding a 'Good Morning.' to Mr Thompson, the baker, as he crossed the square after a hearty breakfast at the inn, he set forth up the lane.

Having walked far enough along to be out of sight of the village, it was time to leave the beaten track and get into the woods proper. The dense undergrowth seemed impenetrable; everything was just intertwined barring his way with nature's natural barrier.

Time to take action and do something rash, he thought. Finding a section that didn't appear to have too many thorns, he tossed his rucksack over - now he was committed, it contained his lunch. Checking again that no-one could see him, he took a step back and then lunged forwards like a diver off the high board.

Timothy rolled to a halt on the soft bed of leaves and scented pine needles. Getting to his feet, he was both surprised and relived that he appeared to be totally unscathed. He picked up his rucksack and quickly secreted himself behind a tree to check out his surroundings. The wood was like any other, the usual tall trees forming an interwoven canopy above. Angled beams of light broke through in patches, warming up the mulch just enough to make steam rise in an ethereal fashion. It was nature's cathedral on an epic scale.

The ground itself, was soft and undulating, like gentle rolling waves with the sweet smell of musty compost rising from underfoot. Here and there, islands of low foliage had formed, taking advantage of stray pools of sunlight. Varieties of ferns rolled out coiled leaves to their best advantage whilst Holly bushes waited patiently for autumn, Timothy however, couldn't wait, he had work to do.

He wasn't good at nature in the raw, he didn't know one plant from another unless it was in a pot with a label. If he'd been asked 'what type of tree is that?' he'd simply answer 'a wooden one.' This could be a hindrance to finding his way around within the wood. Without firm points of reference, he would have difficulty finding the same spot again. Getting lost wasn't too much of a worry; a straight line would always lead him to the outer edge. What would have been useful, was the compass he didn't have.

He stuck a stick in the ground. Timothy was pleased with his solution. He had carved a small notch on it, indicating where he had entered the wood. The hole in the hedgerow had already healed up.

Keeping to what he thought was a reasonably straight line, he cautiously moved on. By his calculations, the little house he'd seen would be on his right-hand side about half-way in, not that he knew where halfway was. His attention was drawn by the sound of trickling water. A tiny stream flowed off to his right. He left another notched stick and followed it deeper into the interior. After a few hundred yards, the little stream disappeared into a pipe at the edge of a dirt track lane. On the other side, stood a tall flint wall that presumably marked the boundary of the Stonely estate. Timothy was confused, the lane must lead up to the cottage he was looking for but where did it begin? Not in the lane he started in, that was for sure.

Not wanting to approach so openly, he back-tracked to his last marker deeper in the woods and carried on north with the intension of coming up behind it.

As he got closer, he happened across what was either a small river or a large stream. Again, Timothy's lack of country knowledge forbade him the answer. He carried on north along its steep banks. Something clicked in his mind, he had heard mention of something called Riverside Cottage, it was starting to make sense now. After a while, he found it.

Although it looked to be part of the estate, it was clearly separated from it by the boundary wall. It was also just perhaps a little reminiscent of something from a Grimm's fairy tale. The neat little building stood isolated in a clearing, a circle of natural light gave it a gentle illumination that was pleasing to the eye. It also marked the end of the lane. The cottage seemed deserted but not disused - just waiting. It probably belonged to the estate gamekeeper. It did have all the elements required for a brewery: fresh running water, ample fuel for a fire and most of all, out of sight of passers-by, bird watchers being a rare exception. Timothy was getting quite excited now and knew he wanted a closer look and that meant crossing the stream. Keeping low, he looked for a narrow crossing point further upstream and came across a crude plank bridge that led into another much smaller open space. Dashing across, he hid himself behind a large earthen mound, one of many that surrounded this otherwise empty clearing.

Timothy's excitement was starting to peak to an almost explosive level. The mound was actually a weathered, moss-covered canvas sheet, perfect camouflage. Cautiously, he scraped away the debris that was holding down the bottom edge and eased it up, the excitement was almost too much but was quickly doused. Timothy had discovered a log pile.

After carefully crawling around and examining the other mounds, he came to the conclusion it was a wood yard for the estate which was more or less confirmed when he spotted a small gateway in the boundary wall of the estate opposite and a wheelbarrow stacked with split logs and kindling.

Deflated, he set off back over the bridge to the relative safety of the woodland. The hidden cottage had been a find and he didn't completely dismiss the possibility of it being a brewery of sorts. It was the nearest Timothy had come to a discovery. He needed time to think and decided to try to find a secluded position where he could watch and have lunch. He wandered off and fell down a hole.

A hundred yards away, a bush was trembling with barely-suppressed laughter.

The hole wasn't deep, which was a good thing, sadly it wasn't dry, which wasn't. Timothy stood momentarily, waist deep in the murky water before scrambling out and scurrying off into some undergrowth and sliding down a small embankment on the other side into a cleft in the ground. He had just entered Jacks Bottom.

Timothy stared ahead in amazement. The annoyance of getting wet faded from his mind as he looked at the device before him. It was a still.

He popped his head up and looked around furtively. All was quiet. His heart was beating nineteen to the dozen with excitement. He had read all the notes that filtered through work and knew what a still was and how it worked and this was defiantly a still, small, crude but functional. The question was, was it still used and how did it fit in with the cottage brewery?

Careful not to touch anything, he took some pictures and sketched the items with some skill just in case the photographs didn't come out. Not that he dared have them sent away for processing locally. He then recorded as best he could its location on his sketch map. There were few signs of use, although the copper piping had tarnished badly to the extent of turning green, the setup was intact and water still ran over the coil. A shelf had been dug out to hold a receiving container but there was no ash under the large kettle but that was probably brushed into the stream after each brew.

As soundlessly as possible, Timothy scrambled out of the cleft and half crouching and half running. He set off towards a holly bush a hundred or so yards distant, he'd planned to set up an observation post here and - observe. Stopping frequently to listen for signs of life, he scooped out a hollow behind the bush to allow himself a low and comfortable position. He was happy that it afforded him a view of the hollow cleft containing the still but also the cottage in the far distance whose previous innocence he now doubted.

It was after he had settled himself down, that he remembered he was still sodden from the waist down. Emptying his rucksack, he spread his plastic raincoat out and proceeded to remove the clothes from his lower half and carefully, crawling on his hands and knees, spread them flat out in a patch of sunlight a few feet away.

The trembling bush had since moved off.

A couple of hours had passed and nothing of interest had happened and Timothy was getting very bored. He had resisted opening his lunch, he knew he was going to be there for a long time and had been making little deals with himself, forcing himself to wait fifteen minutes between moving a limb to a better position, scratching an itch or rolling onto his side. Each involved peeling his naked flesh quietly off his rubber Macintosh. He gave up.

Opening up his rucksack, he extracted his packed lunch. It was the usual door-step sandwich and bottle of beer, courtesy of Clifford. Pickles Pale Ale was far more inviting than the Cow Pat Porter it was replacing. Timothy had paid close attention to the delivery, one barrel in, one barrel out; all was well at the inn. Easing the top off the bottle, he poured away half of the contents, a habit he had now formed after his first experience of bottled beer from Clifford - he intended to keep awake.

He digested the sandwich whilst washing it down with sips of beer. He had rather stupidly assumed Pickles Ale was the name of brewery, it turned out to be the flavour.

Timothy had also come to realise that he didn't have to pay too much attention to the still or cottage either, thanks to the bird life. Any movement and the birds stopped chirping, a brilliant natural early warming system of anything approaching.

Another hour passed and cramp kept attacking his legs. Spasms forced him to stretch out his leg and breathe through gritted teeth, whilst the muscle tensioned with a vice-like grip.

Timothy was reaching his limit, his thoughts were turning on themselves finding reasons not to stay any longer, he knew they'd win but he put up a valiant effort, playing the martyr for a little while longer.

Eventually he caved in, his underwear and trousers now completely dry, he packed up. The still was evidence itself that it was rarely used; clearly a concoction of junk not designed for anything more than a short life, almost an experiment, a kitchen science kit. He would return another day, he'd know if it had been used or moved in any way from the sketches he'd made. Unknown to him, he was four years too late. He decided to take one last look, just in case he'd missed something obvious like a foot print, he had noted that farmers had a wide range of boots and shoes, some held together with little more than string or bailing-twine to stop the sole flapping - one chap even had a miss-matched pair, both left feet. They would all leave a unique cast but sadly there were none.

Timothy wedged a couple of twigs next to the kettle so that he'd know for sure if anyone had been there. Job done, he stepped back to admire his work and lost his footing and fell backwards into the stream. The back of his jacket and trousers were soaked.

It was almost 5 o'clock before he could get dressed again after carefully brushing off the now-dried mud. His return back to the lane he had started in was a much simpler process. He climbed up a tree and shinned along a low, overhanging branch which deposited him as gently as putting eggs in a basket. As he reached the end of the lane opposite the inn, the heavens opened up and a torrent of rain poured down quickly soaking Timothy to the skin.

'Got caught did you?' asked Clifford, as he stepped inside. Timothy was momentarily lost for words.

'The rain.' He added.

'Yes, the rain, caught, yes.' was the best he could manage.

Shirley walked past and winked at him over Clifford's shoulder.

He turned and trudged off to his room, he had a nagging suspicion Shirley knew something about his mostly trouser-less day.

Locking the door, he stripped and dried himself. He was close to giving up, nothing he did seemed to work, and he somehow just managed to embarrass himself at every turn. He had, of course, discovered the still in the woods, that was a plus point but during his hours of observation, it dawned on him that this small isolated bit of equipment was trivial by Customs and Excise standards.

After dinner, he decided he needed to up the game. Rather than just search the countryside, he realised he had to mingle with the village folk themselves and spending the evenings in his room wasn't going to help. Of late, he had forced himself to spend an hour in the bar, reading and melting into the background as much as he could. It hadn't been easy at first, he felt all eyes were upon him, he was the outsider but he strangely felt comfortable in the surroundings. It was now time to come out of his shell.

'You the bird watcher chappie?' asked the old gentleman who stood before Timothy.

'Yes, that's right, just a bit of a hobby really.'

'Names Thwaites, call me Alwyn, bit keen on the birds myself.'

'Oh really.' said Timothy, feigning interest as Alwyn put his pint down on the table and sat on Timothy's right hand side. The next hour was spent discussing the habitat and breeding seasons of the local feathered inhabitants.

'So, what do you do when you're not watching our feathered friends?' asked Mr. Thwaites casually.

'Oh nothing interesting, just a filing clerk in a boring office I'm afraid, imports and exports sort of thing, very dull.' answered timothy, as he drained his glass and was looking for a polite way to bring the conversation to an end.

'Let me get you another, young man.' offered Alwyn swiftly taking Timothy's glass and turning his back on him before he could decline.

At the bar, Alwyn put down the two empty pint glasses and Clifford picked up the first.

'Same again Alwyn?' Alwyn nodded and leaned slightly forward.

'Well?' asked Clifford in a lowered voice.

'He has a passable knowledge of birds alright.'

'Anything else?'

'Not yet, just softening him up a bit.'

'Need a hand?' Clifford winked.

'Worth a try.' replied Alwyn, with a knowing look.

Clifford took Timothy's empty glass and just under the bar, turned on the 'special' tap above the sink and added a small measure of a dark red liquid which he then topped with today's beer, 'Beetroot Bitter' from the hand pump. Pickles Pale Ale, despite its preservative-based ingredients had gone off.

Timothy had had time to think. This old chaps interest in birds was real enough but he was starting to think that he was being tested, some of the things he had said to Timothy were blatantly wrong and Timothy had politely corrected him, silly things but only things a bird watcher would know for sure. Timothy had initially put this down to Alwyn's age. He was grateful that he had studied his bird books carefully. His guard was now up, he had spent a long time getting the bird watcher story right that he had forgotten to have a credible back up story covering his 'normal' everyday work life. He decided to take the initiative, rather than the defensive, in a hope of fending off too many enquiries.

'Here you go, young man' said Alwyn, sitting down and putting the glasses down on the table.
'Have you lived in the village long?' asked Timothy. Alwyn remained staring at the pint glass in front of him. Timothy's glass had been in Alwyn's right hand when he left the bar but he'd made a fatal error, he had sat down first instead of putting the glasses down when he reached the table. This meant the glass that should have been Timothy's was now in front of him.
'Sorry, drifted off for a moment there, what did you say?' answered Alwyn, thinking frantically how he could swap the glasses back without him noticing, they were both drinking the same thing, except his wasn't spiked of course.
Timothy picked up the pint in front of him and asked again if he had lived in the village long whilst taking a long pull on his pint.
'Man and boy' Alwyn answered eventually. 'Man and boy'. Alwyn had no choice but to keep to the same slow drinking pace as Timothy in case he went to the toilet and he could swap the glasses back. He didn't. The next half hour went very slowly, Alwyn seemed to have slipped into introspective mode and happily answered anything Timothy asked, without question. Timothy learned of the history of the village from medieval chalk mining for making quick lime to the present Duke, or 'The Major' as he preferred be known. The history of Stonely Hall was fascinating but the real gem was the absurd will of the Duchess of Stonely and the present Dukes or Majors non-inheritance. The Majors time was almost up and the estate would pass on to this rather loathsome Smallpott character. When pressed for more up-to-date details, Alwyn became less responsive. 'Can't

say any more, hush-hush, you know,' said Alwyn, trying to tap the side of his nose, missed and poked himself in the eye.

Unusually, Timothy insisted on another beer and took the glasses back to the bar. He was intrigued and wanted to know more, he was so pleased he was 'doing his job' at last.

'Same again Timmy?' asked Clifford, taking the first glass.

'Yes please, back in a moment', he answered and went off to the toilet. Clifford looked up and caught Alwyn nodding his head. Clifford took this as a sign to add another drop of tongue loosener to Timothy's pint. Actually Alwyn was nodding off.

When he got back, Clifford placed the pints on the bar so the doctored one would be in Timothy's right hand. Years of experience had taught him that if you're carrying two pints it's usually the one in the left hand that's offered to the other person. Once a pint is in the right hand of a right-handed person, it tended to stay there. Unfortunately for Alwyn and Clifford, Timothy also sat down first before placing the glasses on the table. Timothy was enjoying himself now, the bar was half-full and a gentle hubbub filled the air, no-one took any notice of the two blokes slowly getting drunk in a corner of the comfortable saloon.

It was just coming up to midnight and the bar had closed. Both Timothy and Alwyn were sound asleep, leaning on each other. Timothy didn't need a spiked drink, three beers that evening had done the trick. Alwyn hadn't gained any answers for Clifford as to his background, on the other hand, Timothy had learnt a lot about the village and its people.

'Wake up Timmy.' said Shirley shaking his shoulder, 'time for bed.' Timothy didn't stir.

'That's a first.' laughed Cliff from behind the bar.

'Never been turned down before.' she smiled back.

'I'll get Alwyn home, can you look after him, girl?' asked Clifford.

'Yes sure, I'll tuck him up nice and snug'

It was with some effort, that Shirley got Timothy to stand, his eyes fluttered open for a moment but he decided it was too much effort working his legs at the same time.

'For Christ's sake, don't tie a ribbon around his cock like the last drunk you put to bed, he'd though he'd won a prize when he woke up in the morning.' called Clifford as he lumbered out the front door with Alwyn.

'Spoil-sport.' replied Shirley.

In the Chatterley suite, Shirley let Timothy drop across the bed, he was well out of it. She started to examine the room a little closer. On the bedside table a book of birds, car key and a wallet. This caught her attention. Making sure Timothy was still devoid of consciousness, she opened it up and examined the contents. A library card confirmed he really was a Timothy, and a Montague too boot. There was some cash, loose change and a driving licence also in the name of Montague. She opened up his sketch pad and found drawings of birds, they were surprisingly good. She flipped through and found the map sketch, there was a cross marked where Jacks Bottom was, she assumed it was a good bird watching position, she didn't know about the still.

Shirley turned her attention back to Timothy who remained sparked out. She rolled him over and took off his jacket and shirt; he groaned but didn't open his eyes. Next, she removed his shoes and socks, undid his trousers and rolled him over face down. A gentle tug and they were off, dragging his pants with them.

Shirley looked at his naked bottom for a while, resisting the urge to smack it and smiled. Sliding his underwear back on, she turned him onto his side. She then took his clothes and scattered them around the room, she knew if they were neatly-folded, he would know she had put him to bed.

Happy that everything was in disorder, she took a last look at a very vulnerable young man. Timothy, although of slight build, wasn't without form and Shirley, unable to resist answering one personal question, pulled down the front of his pants, it flopped out.

'My my Timothy, you win first prize'. With the care of someone putting a baby bird back in its nest, Shirley scooped Timothy's flaccid organ back in place a little reluctantly.

'He's Customs & Excise,' said Clifford from behind the bar as Shirley came down the stairs.

'How'd you know?'

'Bookmark.' he answered, pointing to Timothy's bird watching book that still sat on the table.

Shirley walked over and picked up the book, sure enough, a Customs & Excise identity card in the name of Timothy Montague was between the pages.

'The Government must be scraping the bottom of the barrel, unless he's a brilliant actor.' said Clifford.

'Somehow I don't think he's acting, I mean, we've never actually asked what he did for a living have we?, He could really be a bird watcher when not working?'

'Bit of a coincidence though.'

'We've known worse.' replied Shirley, with a rye smile.

'Well, let's just be a little cautious shall we? I have to admit, I quite like the lad and he's taken a fancy to you.'

'I'll use my feminine charms on him shall I?' said Shirley, trusting her bosom forward.

'They've never failed yet.' laughed Cliff.

Chapter 11: Friday in the village

Timothy was up bright and early the next morning - sadly, his head wasn't as keen. The discovery of his pants being on backwards didn't help either, as he fumbled for the fly that wasn't where it was supposed to be.

Having freshened up and dressed properly, he made his way down the creaky stairs to breakfast and there, on the table, where he had become accustomed to sitting, was his bird watching book. He remembered taking it into the bar last night and memories of Alwyn started to come back. He flipped it open and it came to rest where the bookmark lay, Timothy's mouth gaped open.

'Seen a ghost, have we?' asked Clifford, as he placed the breakfast plate before him with its now traditional moat of glistening lard.
Timothy snapped the book closed quickly.

'Sorry, just a bit queasy this morning, I think I had a bit too much to drink last night.' he replied.

'Well at least you managed to get yourself off to bed - that's more than Alwyn did.'

'Oh really?'

'Yep, ended in the wrong house.'

'Oh no . . . whose . . . ' tailed off Timothy.

'The dogs, he'll be in there a while, I should imagine.' Clifford laughed. Get this down you lad, you'll be right as rain after,'

Timothy doubted it.

'I didn't know if that was your book or Alwyn's?' he called over his shoulder as he walked away.

'Oh yes it's mine - thank you.' Timothy relaxed a little. If Clifford had seen his identity-card bookmark, he would have known it wasn't Alwyns'. Luckily, it hadn't been sticking out of the pages. Normally, he would have used a beer mat to mark his position and his ID card stayed securely in his pocket at all times. Instinctively, he ran his hand over his trouser pocket and sure enough, he could feel the shape of a beer mat. He ate his breakfast in slow reflection, trying to put some order to the events of last night. He would have to be more careful in future. Out of sight, Clifford smiled to himself.

Breakfast over, Timothy retreated back to the safety of his room to gather his thoughts together and plan what to do next. He'd been investigating now for almost a week with no real evidence of anything that would interest the department. He hadn't sent in a report either but he felt justified as the only telephone was in the post office and any letters might be steamed open.

'Take as long as you feel necessary.' were the words the department head had said, was a week long enough he wondered, and do spies get the weekends off?

His thoughts were interrupted by the unmistakable sound of a large vehicle pulling up outside. Timothy looked out of the bedroom window to see it wasn't the usual one from the brewery but a battered farm lorry with a canvas sheet over its load. Clifford, the landlord, appeared below and spoke to the driver for a moment and then moved along the side lifting up a corner of the cover to inspect the load. Timothy caught sight of some empty beer bottles in crates. Things were looking up. As quickly as he could, he got himself together, grabbed his back-pack and almost stumbled down the stairs as he heard the vehicle drive off. He was just reaching for the door handle, when it was abruptly opened by a rather stout ruddy-faced gentleman with a military bearing.

'Hello, you must be the bird watcher chap?'

'Yes, indeed.' replied Timothy, as he watched the lorry disappear down the road over the strangers shoulder.

'This is His Grace, the Duke of Stonely.' said Clifford, who was standing behind him.

'Call me Major, no need to stand on ceremony here.'

'Major, a pleasure to meet you sir.' Timothy's heart was sinking but social politeness was a must and this was the closest he would ever come to royalty. He clasped the outstretched hand and received a firm hearty shake. It was unusually hard-skinned, implying some sort of manual labour which struck Timothy as a little odd for a titled country gentleman, especially a Duke.

'Good good, you must have a look around the estate sometime, we have some wonderful peacocks roaming about, not native of course, but a sight to behold.'

'Yes, I'd like that very much.' replied Timothy, who actually would.

'Well I mustn't keep you, I'm sure we'll bump into each other again on Sunday.'

'Yes indeed, Sunday, look forward to it.' finished Timothy and strode out the door. Hmm… Sunday, that was a bit cryptic he thought, or would have, had he known what the word meant. Was it an invitation to visit the estate? It didn't sound like it. People like the Major would usually make things like that very clear and besides, when people use the word 'sometime', it's rarely followed through, it's an offer that's never expected to be taken up.

Striding purposely down the lane, trying his best to look as casual as possible, Timothy hunted for clues to where the lorry might have gone. Although the lane didn't have any roads joining it, it had plenty of gates in the tall summer hedgerows surrounding the fields that could easily hide a lorry within. Of course, it could have just left the area completely and joined the main road some five miles away. As it happened, it hadn't. Only two fields down the lane, Timothy spotted its tail end behind a stack of baled hay, one of many around the field.

Paying no obvious attention, Timothy strolled on past until he felt he was a suitable distance away and looked for an entrance into the adjacent field. There was none.

Forcing himself through the hedgerow whose very core seemed to be made of thorns, he tumbled out on to the grass on the other side, rolling for several feet.

Remaining prone for a moment, he removed a thorn from his thigh and flicked it ahead of him. It was then, he noticed two farmhands in the far distance handling what looked like ropes and coloured flags. Timothy went rigid; he'd stumbled upon the makings of something secret, was it a makeshift runway? So, that was their game! There must be really good money in illicit brewing. For a moment, he wondered what would happen if he were caught. He wouldn't be able to stand up to any interrogation, he had a vision of his body being beaten and buried in a shallow grave in the woods, never to be seen again. This worried Timothy, he already had an over-due library book as it was.

Using just his elbows and toes, he levered himself along the ground and headed back from whence he came, finally emerging back out in the lane. He risked a look back, the farm hands seemed totally oblivious of anything other than the job in hand.

Brushing himself down, he stood in the lane wondering what to do next. He had to pick a direction quickly before someone came along. Going up the hill wouldn't be a good idea, there was only sparse cover near the top and he'd be easily spotted from the field below. He started to walk away to give himself some thinking time, when he heard the sound of a car approaching from behind at speed.

Moving closer to the verge, he carried on, hoping it would just pass him by. The horn sounded and the Major's Bentley pulled up beside him.

'Got something for you, young man.' said the Major reaching over to the passenger seat. Timothy hesitantly turned towards the car and saw the shotgun resting upright against the passenger door. The Major reached over towards it and brought up a brown paper parcel. Timothy's first thought was hush money. He took the package. It was soft and smelt of bacon.

'Clifford wasn't sure if you were in for lunch, he left out the beer, said that you probably had enough last night.' he laughed, as he put the gently throbbing engine into gear. 'Can I drop you off anywhere?'

'Thank you Major, I'm fine, thank you.' The car glided off with little effort and was soon out of sight. Timothy meanwhile, had wet himself.

Timothy had decided to go up the hill after all, his plan was to circle around the back and peek over the top. His first action however, was sorting himself out down below. He couldn't recall any of his fictional heroes wetting themselves whilst staring death in the face.

He remembered the small stone ruin a little way up the path to the hill that had a small trickling brook within its bounds; here he could rinse out his trousers and pants. They should dry quickly in the warm sunshine.

Having carefully climbed over the stone wall that surrounded the ruin and going out of sight around the back, he undressed from the waist down and proceeded to rinse out his soiled underwear and trousers in the brook. Wringing them firmly out, like his mother used to do, he spread them out on the warm stone wall. Remembering he'd left his rucksack against the front wall, he quickly nipped around the front and leaned over and picked it up.

'Hello there.' came a voice from a distance. For the second time that day, Timothy froze. It was Shirley, walking down the path with what looked like a large wicker basket in her hand. Timothy daren't move. At the moment the wall between him and the approaching Shirley was just high enough to hide his naked bottom half.

'What are you up to then?' asked Timothy, in as nonchalant a way as possible as she drew level.

'Oh, just picking some wild mushrooms for dinner tonight, and you?'

Just the usual, you know' he relied shifting his weight from one leg to the other. He could feel himself being bitten.

'I'd like to join you but I've got to get these back before they go too limp.' She smiled and started to move off.

Limp wasn't a problem Timothy was having. He remained where he was, pretending to scan the skies for birds, incredibly conscious of his nakedness and how stupid he must look. How was it that Shirley always managed to pop up when he had his trousers down?

Once she was out of sight, he gingerly nipped around the back of the ruin, cursing himself. His pants were gently steaming; he hoped she hadn't spotted them on the far wall.

'Ouch.' he uttered, another bite, enough was enough, he was going to get dressed in damp clothes rather than be a feast for the insect life.

It was a couple of hours later when Timothy had finally navigated his way around the back of the hill and eased himself up to the top. The view was, as always - stunning. His past trips here hadn't been this far up. From here, he could see the valley formed by this and the hill on the other side and only a few feet below was a large flat plateau, where presumably Stonely castle one stood proud. Sure enough, there was a sunken area within and the odd stone block scattered here and there.

His view over the land below was now clear. He could see the field with the baled hay and the lorry seemed to be untouched. Farmhands were slowly taking the bails down and building some sort of wall arrangement, which was odd. It was then, that Timothy saw the real treasure, beer barrels and lots of them, now being exposed as the straw was removed. They had been hidden there all the time - how clever.

The adjacent field where the makeshift runway was being made, now had three clear white lines marked from one end to the other, he could now see that the ropes were used as a guide for a hand-pushed roller that painted the whitewash lines on the grass, the same thing he'd seen at his old school playing-field, marked out for football matches.

Timothy watched as one chap started pacing one of the lines and placing a small flag every three steps. Through the binoculars, it looked like each flag had a number on, obviously a guide for the pilot. Possibly a night-landing, he'd need every help to land in that field, it wasn't very long. Timothy sketched the layout of the two fields and their map positions.

Deciding not to tempt fate too much, he returned to the safety of the other side of the hill and out of sight of the village and the fields. Unpacking his lunch of a fried crispy bacon omelette sandwich, he started to try to look at things from a different direction, what if . . .

'What if . . .' he said out loud, '. . . There was no brewery?' His mind went racing ahead, stalled and waited for him to catch up. 'What if this was a delivery, beer was arriving, not leaving, no brewery, ha.' It would, in Timothy's mind, explain why those bottles on the lorry were empty. The beer would be pumped into the waiting barrels and then bottled at their leisure or just simply swapped over like a milkman collecting the empties.

Pleased with his deductions, he allowed a broad grin to cross his face. What everyone thought was a small illicit brewery of little real interest, just an exercise for the new boy, turned out to be a part of a far greater operation, not a small cog but a major gear wheel. He allowed himself to be smug for a while. However, doubt stared to creep in, it was an awful lot of trouble just for beer, there must be something else as well, something of far greater value? Diamonds, gold, perfume, silk, cigarettes even, from the continent! We were close to the south coast here, an easy flight for a small aircraft. Coast guards watched the waters, he knew that well, but nothing could watch the skies efficiently, not all aircraft land at airports.

Timothy made his way slowly back down the hill and into the village, it was now mid-afternoon and he had a lot of thinking to do. He had been on the verge of giving up but things were very different, it was getting exciting, and dangerous remembering the major's shotgun and wetting himself.

Back in the safety of his locked room, he stripped off to his underwear - he was starting to itch quite badly now. Timothy stood closer to the window, whilst remaining behind the net curtain. It was here, in good light, that he noticed the little round grey lumps on his legs the size and shape of shelled peas. He squeezed one and it burst with a pop and a splash of blood.

After a few moments he came to. He couldn't believe he'd fainted. Thankfully, it was onto the bed and not the floor. Raising his leg to examine the spot, he saw that the little sack of burst skin was now flat and flabby but something else was happening. As he looked closer, he could make out little legs and they were moving. This thing was sucking his blood and it wasn't alone.

Dr Strange was, as his name implied – a little odd.

'It's good of you to see me so quickly, Doctor.' said Timothy.

'Not a problem, dear boy, not a problem, been doing a lot of walking in long grass have we?' asked the Doctor, examining Timothy's rolled-up trouser leg.

'Yes I'm a bird watcher, I'm afraid' said Timothy, almost as if an apology were needed.

'Sheep ticks, blood sucking little bastards, I'd Like to say they're harmless.'

'Harmless?' repeated Timothy.

'Yes I'd like to say that, can't of course, little shits.'

'How not-harmless, are they?' enquired Timothy with the slightest of quavers in his voice.

'Kills sheep sometimes, sends 'em round the bend.'

'Oh . . .'

'Don't worry, I'll give you some antibiotics, you'll come to no harm.' Timothy visibly relaxed.

'How many do you think you have on your legs then?' asked Dr Strange.

'Just the three well, two now.'

'Doubt it' said the Doctor, 'these things like to hide, cracks, creases and hair.'

Timothy went pale. The doctor looked up at him over his half moon glasses. 'You'd better strip off and I'll get something to remove them with.' With that, he left the room.

Timothy reluctantly stood up off the stool and stripped off. This would be the third time today. He sat back down on the stool and risked a glance down at his pubic hair, he thought he saw movement and was almost sick.

A minute or two later, the doctor returned with what looked like a teaspoon with a small 'V' shaped groove cut in the front and a pair of scissors.

'If you'd like to have a bit of a trim down there,' he said handing Timothy the scissors, 'my hands aren't as steady as they used to be, wouldn't want me cutting your knob off now, would we?'

Timothy tended to agree and set about his first hair dressing experience with caution.

'The secret is getting underneath, twisting the little bugger first to get its teeth out and then flicking it out.' carried on the doctor, with some relish.

'That's eleven then, young man, good thing we looked isn't it?' finished Dr Strange, as he injected the antibiotic in his arm.

Timothy had never been so embarrassed, nothing had been left to chance, every crack and crease had been explored, his head hair thoroughly combed, in fact he was surprised he hadn't been sheep dipped. Timothy returned to the inn, this was one time that a pint would be really welcome.

'Hello, Pint of whatever's on tap today, please Cliff.'

'Mellow Marrow, Timmy, it will take your mind off those sheep ticks I bet.' answered Clifford, in a jovial manner. There was muted laughing from the shadows.

'How'd you know?' said Timothy, who had become resigned to the fact that everyone knew what everyone else was doing or going to do.

'It's the cream old Strange puts on afterwards, smell it a mile away, we've all been there believe me, sack and crack. Best to tuck your trousers in your socks from now on matey.' finished Clifford, putting the pint down in front of him.

Just then, Shirley appeared behind the bar, 'Hello Timothy, You been to see . . . '

'Yes.'

'Bless.'

Timothy took a long hard pull on the pint and savoured its interesting but not unpleasant taste, he then wandered over to the window seat and lent back and relaxed.

'Remember when old man Parker went to the doc's because he thought he had piles?' said one of the shadows.

'Ah yes, turned out they were ticks if I remember.' replied Clifford.

'Serves him right, taking a shit in my field,' laughter broke out and a chorus of aye's followed.

Timothy smiled, there was nothing quite like relaxing after work in a country pub, it was something he was becoming accustomed to, although he couldn't really call this work. He started to run through his mind the events of the day. The beer barrels, the makeshift airfield, wetting himself at the sight of a shotgun, of course the Major wasn't going to shoot him, that's just silly. He knew something was up but no one seemed to take a blind bit of notice, life just carried on and Cliff called him Timmy, in fact, everyone did. He was starting to feel that he not only had their trust, but that somehow he'd earned it. The last thing he wanted to do was cause trouble, it just didn't seem right, he was growing to like the people and he felt he had become accepted, not even a full week had passed.

Chapter 12 An Ornithologist Arrives

'Afternoon landlord, William Roystone, I'm looking for a room for a week or two, do you have one?'

'Yes sir, I think we can just about fit you in, five pounds a week, all in.' replied Clifford.

'Ideal, thank you.'

'Bird watcher, are you?'

'My goodness, how did you know?' answered Roystone, feigning surprise'.

'Well, you actually look like one.' smiled Clifford.

'Funny you should say that, just doing a little research for my latest book on countryside ornithology, as it happens. You get a lot of bird watchers around here then?'

'No none at all, you're the second this month, other than that . . . never.'

'How odd.' smiled Roystone.

'Yes, isn't it?' replied Clifford, who was starting to warm to him. Fancy a pint? first one's on the house!'

'How could I refuse?'

'The other chap's called Montague, Timothy Montague, been here nearly a week, out most of the day . . . watching.'

'Well, you do have some delightful scenery roundabouts, and so secluded, an advantage I should imagine. Perhaps I'll bump into Mr. Montgomery later and we'll bore each other to death.'

Clifford laughed out loud, he liked Mr. Roystone.

'We have another guest, a Mr Roystone, he's in the Canterbury suite,' said Clifford to Shirley later that afternoon, 'and this one's a real bird watcher, writing a book about it.'

'Well if he can write, then he must be a real one,' said Shirley, with a hint of sarcasm.

'This one has the proper credentials, leather patches on the elbows, frayed shirt cuffs, scuffed shoes and none of his luggage is new.' Even Shirley had to admit that this added a level of credibility.

Upstairs, William Roystone was looking down at his shoes whilst he tamped down the fresh tobacco in his pipe. He'd hated roughing up a decent pair of shoes, almost as much as ruining his favourite tweed jacket gardening but it was a necessary means to an end. He lit his pipe with a silver Ronson lighter and looked briefly at the words engraved on one side.

The cherry-wood aroma soon removed that strange but not unpleasant aftertaste of marrow that had appeared on his palette.

Timothy Montgomery - now he knew the full name of his bird watching counterpart. He would enjoy bumping into him later and testing his cover. His own was of course perfect, he was writing a book on British birds and their habitat after his modest success with 'Birds of Asia' and so his cover was foolproof, as was his knowledge.

He had been fascinated with the village so intentionally devoid of directions to or from. He had very quickly understood the benefits of remaining a closed circle, the past war would not even have been an inconvenience, the land suggested that it was self supporting and kept itself to itself.

Now the Duke of Stonely, or 'The Major,' as he preferred to be known, did interest Roystone a great deal. But that was by-the-by, he was here to investigate Reginald Smallpott and the Major was his present employer.

He didn't unpack, it was a habit he had got into when working. There had been the odd occasion when he had to move on quickly, leaving his luggage behind. The attached leather tag, when opened, had a PO box number written on half of a 10 pound note, this seemed to ensure its safe return.

After making some notes in his pocket diary, he spent the rest of the afternoon leisurely watching the world go by out of the bedroom window. He had no need to explore any further, he had already spent a week in the woods disguised as a bush.

Early evening and he decided it was time to meet the people who made up the village folk and the bar seemed a good place to start, it saved so much time in these cases.

'You must be Timothy?' said Roystone.

'Yes.' said Timothy, rising slightly from the bench to shake the outstretched hand.

'William Roystone - we share a common interest I believe.'

'We do?'

'Birds . . . the study thereof.'

'Oh yes, you're a bird watcher then?'

'I Prefer ornithologist, just started my study of British Birds of the Countryside, it's the title of my next book.'

'Oh.' smiled Timothy weakly, an author and an authority, he thought to himself, aware that this could be his undoing as he glanced over Mr. Roystone's shoulder to see who might be listening. He knew he could pass muster with the average watcher now but an expert, this was a different kettle of fish.

'It's wonderful to be able to get out and about isn't it? at one with nature.' carried on Mr. Roystone, who remained standing.

Roystone already knew Timothy wasn't who he was pretending to be, by his antics in the woods and surrounding area. Now he just had to work out why. He toyed with the idea of taking him to task but thought better of it. Timothy obviously had something to hide and would naturally become defensive and that would achieve little other than shutting doors. No, he would remain unchallenging and comfortably friendly; it would suit his character and protect Timothy's. He was also fully aware that others were listening. William Roystone was starting to enjoy himself.

'May I?' he asked, indicating the empty space next to Timothy.

'Yes of course, please do.' replied Timothy with rising panic and budged up slightly on the padded bench under the window. Roystone could have sat in the vacant chair opposite but chose the bench purposely. It afforded him a good view of the interior of the inn and the very reason Timothy always sat there and of course it was far less intimidating, a technique he had often used to put people at their ease.

'I'm hoping to catch sight of some hawks and possibly a kestrel or two, have you spotted any?' asked Roystone.

'Yes I have.' answered Timothy, who was on safe ground here, 'Sparrow Hawks, a pair of Marsh Harriers and Kestrels are quite common around here.'

'Marsh Harriers, isn't that a little unusual?' enquired Roystone.

'Oh yes normally but just behind the inn there is some marsh land which is ideal for them, you can sit in the garden out the back and watch them at your leisure.'

'Wonderful, and Kestrels are common you say?

'Yes indeed, there's plenty of open fields about, I like to sit up on the hill and watch from there.' finished Timothy, realising he was giving away his favourite position, then it suddenly dawned on him that this might expose the strange goings on in the fields down the road, the badly hidden barrels and makeshift airfield, he'd almost forgotten about that discovery.

'I would recommend the woodland as well', he added hurriedly.

Sensing he needed to take over the conversation and ease the pressure off Timothy, he started to relate some bird watching stories long enough to satisfy the landlord listening from the bar that 'boring' really did mean boring and he'd lose interest and drift off to chat with the other regulars. He did.

It was an hour or so later, that Reginald Smallpott entered the inn. A hush fell over the room. Roystone however, carried on chatting but watched Timothy's interest in the new customer, it was clear that he didn't know who he was. He, on the other hand, did.

'Mr Smallpott, nice to see you.' said Clifford, as he approached the bar, 'Usual is it?'

'Please Landlord.' answered Smallpott, keeping the formality of customer and servant. It was little wonder no-one took to him.

Shirley appeared behind the bar, 'Hello Mr Smallpott.'

'Ah, hello Shirley, delightful to see you my dear.' Smallpott visibly changed in female company, a gentle bow of the head and smile.

'Down for the weekend then?' she asked, folding her arms across her bosom, whereas normally she would have folded them under to add emphasis to her already naturally buoyant charms.

'Yes indeed, business and pleasure, but one has to take time to relax and enjoy oneself, don't you think?'

The false airs and graces exhibited by someone who wasn't born with them showed up like beetroot stains on a white cotton tablecloth, noticed but politely ignored.

Clifford placed the glass of sherry down in front of Smallpott who offered payment with a new, crisp ten pound note. 'Sorry, smallest.' he said, his demeanour changing instantly now he wasn't addressing a woman.

Even Timothy picked up on this, the rotund little man wasn't at all pleasing to the eye, his hair greased down almost flat, with a centre-parting and so shiny it was almost reflective, he gave the impression of a French waiter, not that Timothy had seen one in the flesh having never travelled out of the country, but an instant dislike was forming.

Smallpott took up a seat near the door, opposite a window almost as if he had selected a position that showed him in his best light, and proceeded to read a copy of the Times that he had brought with him. 'Lording it', was the phrase that came to mind. A natural island formed around him. The rest of the evening in the bar seemed strained, no-one felt they could relax and chat idly. Both Roystone and Timothy opted for sandwiches in the bar rather than eat in the dining room with Smallpott, so it seemed did everyone else.

Later, back in his room, William Roystone sat in the chair and steepled his fingers together. Timothy Montague was interesting, he lacked confidence in almost everything and the clothes he wore were all recently purchased. His knowledge of birds was basic to say the least, and sexually inexperienced too judging by the amount of attention he paid to the flirty barmaid Shirley.

Smallpott, on the other hand, was a closed book. Yes, his demeanour was false, his attitude awful and his pretence at being something he wasn't was almost embarrassing. He liked Reginald Smallpott because he knew he could bring him down, he had so much to lose.

Down the hallway, Timothy sat on his bed trying to contemplate his next move, he didn't have one. The appearance of William Roystone was awkward for his cover but fortunately, he hadn't been put on the spot. In fact, he found himself warming to him. Smallpott was very interesting. The stories he had overheard and from what he'd gleaned from Alwyn, had painted a very dire picture but as it turned out, an accurate one. Not that he had spoken to him, he didn't need to, being in his presence was enough. Timothy did for a moment, wonder if Smallpott was the man behind the beer smuggling ring, Mr. big but that was too far-fetched, even for country standards.

Chapter 13: Burnt Cow Day

Shirley placed Timothy's breakfast down in front of him and asked what he was up to today.

'Nothing planned, thought I might have it off,' he answered innocently.

'Really, anyone in mind?' There was a short pause whilst the alternative meaning sunk in.

'Oh God, no, I didn't mean, sorry' and blushed.

'Well I'm having it off this afternoon too, would you like to join me? It's Burnt Cow Day.'

Timothy gaped, struggling to comprehend the twisted conversation.

'Old Hogget's field at noon, there's something for everyone.' she said with a wink and walked away.

Hogget's field, that's where the barrels were hidden and the airfield, he'd been invited to attend a smuggling operation. This can't be right, how could they be so blatant and so trusting?

Noon arrived and Timothy left the inn for what he thought just might be the last time, perhaps it was the final question, would he join them or . . . he left that unanswered.

The gate to the field was wide open and . . . it was a fete, a bloody village fete.

The bales of straw had been arranged into seating and crude tables. There were benches set up, laden with home made cakes, jams, honey and things he knew must have a name and were probably edible. Just about everybody was here, not just the handful of people he'd met but the whole village, numbering around a hundred or so.

'Timmy.' called the familiar voice of Clifford, the inn's landlord. There were the four barrels he'd seen yesterday in a cleverly made bar constructed of bales.

'It's all free today Timmy, best stick to halves mind you, we've had this maturing for a year and it's a bit heady.'

Clifford offered him a freshly filled bottle of very dark beer with a rich brown head frothing out of the neck, it had a pleasant coffee and chocolate aroma.

'What's it all in aid of, Cliff?' asked Timothy.

'Burnt Cow Day, ah, here comes Shirley, she'll take you in hand', he laughed uproariously.

'Is Shirley married at all?' he asked, trying desperately not to sound interested in the answer.

'Shirley, no . . . she used to be the local bike.'

'Oh, she runs errands for people?'

'Well, let's just say her saddle was always warm.'

Timothy didn't understand, he sensed Clifford was saying something funny but he just didn't get the joke.

'Come with me, young man, I want you to taste my cherry pie.' she said out loud, to even more laughter. Shirley linked her arm with his and led Timothy across the field to a bench absolutely crammed with pastry products, apple pie, blackcurrant pie, apple and blackcurrant pie, game pie, poachers Pie and what looked like the biggest gala pie he'd ever seen. This was like a feast from some medieval banquet. Timothy had trouble focusing on such delights, not just that but Shirley's breast was pressing against his arm and starting to make walking a little problematic with his steadily increasing down-below problem. He still had his binoculars slung across his shoulders and desperately wanted to manoeuvre them around the front to disguise his growing interest but now both hands were full, pint in one hand and cherry pie in the other.

'It's a magnificent spread' he said eventually.

'Yes, a lot of people say that,' she giggled, 'but the real fun starts in half an hour when we play 'Shitting-in-a-Box' in the next field.'

It wasn't possible for Timothy to get any more confused and he almost asked her to repeat what she just said but thought better of it, he was sure he had misheard.

Shirley released her arm from his, 'I'll be back in a minute, have a wander around.' Timothy suddenly felt even more awkward and looked for a place to rest the pie and beer for a moment. He had just made it over to the hand-made wicker basket and trug stall, next to the Penny Roll when there was a hearty slap on his back.

'Well done lad, so glad you could come along, splendid isn't it?' said the Major, who Timothy noted, had his shotgun under his arm. 'You'll try your hand at the trap shoot won't you? you're welcome to borrow my gun, just ask Henderson over there, say I said it was alright.'

Almost on cue, a loud crack followed by another, retorted from the far end of the field. Timothy had been thrown into a world of wonder, surrounded by colour, sounds, and delightful aromas. It was hard to imagine that he would have to eventually go back to dowdy city life. He was starting to feel at home, no one treated him any differently here. He found himself nodding to familiar faces as they passed, they all knew his name but he hardly knew theirs.

Reginald Smallpott was enjoying it too but for different reasons, he wasn't there. He was sat in his little cottage waiting. A bush, by the name of Roystone, observed from a distance.

' . . . and this drunken farmhand set fire to his wedding tackle and ended up burning the whole cow field and we've been having a spit roast every year since.' finished Shirley, who didn't mention the cracked brewery pipe from the Stonely estate or what part, if any, a cow played in it.

Timothy marvelled at the simplicity of the story and the rigidness of Shirley's nipples through her cotton blouse whose reaction was no doubt set off by her holding a cold bottle of beer between them. He took another sip of his beer and surveyed the field before him over the hedge. It was the same one he previously thought was an airfield. Shirley had led him up a steep, wooden ramp onto a grandstand made of straw bails and planks. It overlooked the field, which had been carefully divided up into equal-sized squares, each with a little numbered flag in the top right-hand corners. It was a game, by the looks of it.

'It's a game' confirmed Shirley, 'Two cows are put in the field and you place a bet on one or the other and guess which square it has a shit in, only a penny a square.

Timothy mused for a moment; it was crude but natural in a funny sort of way.

'Do you fancy having a go then? She asked.

'Oh I don't think I could do that, not in public.' he answered.

Shirley looked at him nonplussed, he smiled and she burst in to laughter, 'Oh that was clever, well done. You got me there.' and squeezed Timothy's thigh with her hand. Timothy crossed his legs.

Hoghorn was walking towards Riverside Cottage; she had entered the woods via the little gate built into the estate boundary wall. She had a package under her arm.

As she approached the cottage, the door opened to reveal Smallpott in the doorway. She entered and Smallpott glanced around before retreating inside.

William Roystone slowly melted into the woods and removed his gilly suit. He'd seen all he needed for now.

Back at the fete, Timothy had won half a crown and was very pleased with himself, it had been a close thing, his cow had stood in the wrong square but managed to project the contents of its bowels into another, the one he had chosen. He collected his winnings and a beer came out of nowhere and arrived in his hand.

'Shall we try the trap shoot before you down that one?' suggested Shirley, squeezing his arm. He was putty in her hands, mostly.

At the far end of the field were the traps. Denis Henderson was in charge of this stall. Timothy had seen him in the bar a couple of times but had never spoken, he always seemed to have a friendly nature about him.

'Ever fired a shotgun before, Timothy?' he asked, Timothy didn't even notice that Henderson already knew his name.

'No, can't say that I have, perhaps I'd better leave it for now.'

'No, don't be silly,' egged on Shirley 'Denis will help, have a go.'

A small crowd was gathering, word spread quickly when someone was firing a shotgun for the first time, it was guaranteed a laugh.

'We'll just use one barrel to start with, to be on the safe side.' said Henderson, more to the gathering audience than Timothy. They all knew too well that the kick-back of the first barrel firing on a double barrel, often caused the novice to discharge the second inadvertently.

Timothy listened intently to Henderson's instructions, examined the 'clay' that he would be aiming at, how the gun loaded and where to point it.

'All ready then?' smiled Henderson, again glancing over Timothy's shoulder at the two burly farmhands who had positioned themselves behind to catch him, they nodded. Timothy said yes.

'PULL'

There was a sound, not unlike that of a large catapult and then the light brown saucer shape spun into the air.

Crack, went the gun, the disc shattered into powder and Timothy remained standing upright, much to everybody's surprise and possibly disappointment. A cheer and a round of applause followed.

'Well well, looks like you know how to handle your weapon,' laughed Shirley

'It was my first time, honest.' said Timothy, full of confidence as his thumb clipped the barrel locking-lever. The barrel dropped down, opening the breach and the spent cartridge ejected in an arc in slow-motion, its predicted trajectory was that of Shirley's low-cut bosom-enhancing top.

A hand snatched it in mid air and tossed it harmlessly over the gun bench.

'Thank you Mr. Roystone, good catch.'

'A pleasure Miss.' he replied and strolled off.

Shirley looked at Timothy, 'I'd have made you kiss them better, you know.' she said with a wink.

Chapter 14: A bird in the hand

'And where are you off to today Timothy?' asked Shirley, as she put the brimming breakfast plate before him. He noted the position of the two fried eggs. He was reading more into this than there actually was, and the sausage between them didn't help.

'I thought I'd go up the hill this afternoon, it's a magnificent view, and birds of course,' he added quickly, hoping she didn't think he was implying her cleavage, which he wasn't, but every time he said something to her he could see a smutty side to it, this wasn't like him at all.

Breakfast eaten, Timothy returned to his room to gather his things together. He sorted out his kit, leaving a space for the packed lunch that Clifford would inevitably supply and sat on the edge of the bed watching the village square coming to life through the net curtains; it was then that he noticed a thin pocket book on the window sill he was sure wasn't there the other day.

'A Farmer's Guide to Pig Breeding'. It was an interesting browse but what was striking, were the illustrations. No detail had been omitted from the entire breeding cycle, graphically it was bordering on pornography but because it was a technical manual on animal husbandry it was acceptable. He recalled the day he had gone on a school trip to the zoo and watched monkeys masturbating and no-one paid them any attention, it seemed to be a trait particular to the English: he, on the other hand, learnt a lot that day.

Flipping through the rest of the book, he noticed some of the pages were stuck together, a dark thought crossed his mind which he quickly dismissed. After washing his hands, he gathered together his rucksack and set off for the hills.

It was another beautiful day with clear skies and excellent visibility. His plan was to keep a distant eye on the still he had found in the woods. From a high vantage point, he could easily see anyone approaching the woods from all directions. A far better solution than camping out in the undergrowth, he thought.

As Timothy rounded a gorse bush near the summit, he discovered an almost-naked woman lying on her back on the grass, she was wearing blue shorts and a white lace brassiere; a cotton blouse covered her head.

'Shirley?'

Shirley pulled the blouse off her face and squinted up at Timothy as she raised herself up on her elbows.

'Oh, hello, how did you know it was me?' she smiled.

'I recognised your . . . shoes' replied Timothy, 'I hope I didn't startle you?' he said, trying to avert his eyes from her near nakedness.

'No, I was expecting you, I thought I'd come and see what your fascination is with birds and do a bit of sunbathing at the same time, is that alright, I don't want to be a nuisance?'

'No of course, you're very welcome.' answered Timothy, looking away as Shirley adjusted her bra without making any attempt to cover up. He was a little amazed that something so obviously thin and flimsy managed its job so well, he would have expected something more along the lines of a sturdy harness with brass buckles.

Timothy was naturally uncomfortable around women and semi-naked ones even more so, not that that occurred very often, if at all. It took a while for him to settle down comfortably, trying to concentrate on looking everywhere but directly at Shirley, although admittedly he risked the odd glance now and again.

Later, sharing the packed lunch together, Timothy explained the habits of the bird life that flitted about them.

'And that's a great tit sitting on the fence there,' pointed out Timothy, 'It's the largest of all the tits in Britain.'

'Are these great tits?' asked Shirley.

Timothy turned to discover that Shirley had removed her bra and her bosoms were now free and taking deep breaths. He froze in both awe and panic, an inner urge made him want to get up and run away and hide, this wasn't a teasing glance but a full frontal assort.

'They're . . . magnificent.' he managed.

Shirley giggled and they bounced up and down in response. He went instantly bright red and stirrings started in his underwear. He raised one knee up slightly to hide his fast growing embarrassment.

Then came the awkward pause, he didn't know quite what he should do, this was new ground for him.

'Do they have names?' he asked and realised it was an utterly stupid thing to say and mentally kicked himself. Shirley laughed and her breasts joined in. She inclined her head towards him slightly and said softly, 'You're new at this, aren't you?' Timothy didn't answer, it was after all a foregone conclusion and he managed a small nod and a whimper.

She cupped her breasts and then started to run her fingers teasingly around the expanding nipples. 'Look, they're pleased to see you.' She then put her hand on his raised knee and slid it down and round until it was resting on his crutch and gave it a gentle squeeze.

Timothy let out a little squeal, 'It's a problem I have' he said quickly. 'Oh, it's not a problem Timmy . . . it's a gift.'

'I think that girl needs a raise for what she's doing' said George, the cellar man, who was watching through the telescope from a back window at the inn.
'Oh I think that's in hand', smiled Clifford.

And then she kissed him. Timothy knew that he wanted Shirley there and then. The book on pig breeding had been informative but there were obvious differences, she for example only had two nipples instead of eight and at the moment, she seemed to be trying to force her tongue into his mouth. Timothy was going to lose something that afternoon.

Chapter 15: To kill a Mocking Bird

'We could drown the bastard in a cesspit.' suggested Warren from High Clare farm.

'Or feed him to my pigs, they're not fussy what they eat.' added Mick the Pork.

'Not as simple as that, lads,' interrupted Clifford to the small assembled group in the bar. 'He can't just disappear like that, there has to be a body to prove he's dead and it has to look like an accident to boot.'

'Point is,' chipped in Henderson, 'it mustn't reflect on the Major or any of us that have something to gain from it.'

'We ain't got nuffin to gain from it have we, it's what we gonna lose, he has to go, I don't know how I ain't blessed with them sort of brains.' finish Uncle-dad the inbred.

Timothy was eating his breakfast in the dining room and could overhear the conversation clearly. His mind was racing away, they must have found out who he was working for and now they planned to do away with him, either that or they knew he'd had sex with Shirley, or both. At that moment, Clifford appeared through the doorway with a shotgun in his hand. Timothy sat there transfixed.

'Don't suppose you'd fancy bagging a couple of rabbits while you're out would you?' said Clifford, offering him the gun.

Timothy accepted it automatically, it seemed rude not to, it was a great honour to be trusted with such a thing.

'And if you were to accidentally shoot Smallpott on the way, we'd be much obliged.' he said nodding his head in the direction of the bar and laughed. With that, Clifford gave him a bag of cartridges and his usual sandwiches and beer.

Timothy worried too much and jumped to conclusions at the drop of a hat. It was clear that the village had nothing to hide, other than its own existence. It bothered him that they might find out who he was and he'd be drummed out of the village in a walk of shame. It was now more important than ever, that his secret remained just that, a secret, despite the overwhelming urge to tell Shirley and to try and assure her he was on holiday and that his official 'hat' was at home. That, so far, was the best he had come up with.

Walking up the lane, he now had a purpose. He had to stick to his daily routine of going out 'bird watching' to keep up the pretence but now he had a job to do, hunting rabbits. It didn't occur to him that he'd never killed anything before. It also gave him the opportunity to reflect on the past week and his immediate future.

Sunday had been perhaps the best day of his adult life, socially. The Burnt Cow Festival had shown him how welcoming a close knit community could be. Strangers were usually shunned because they either upset the balance or simply just didn't fit in. He had always been shy and isolated, keeping himself to himself and he knew deep down he wasn't clever or talented but that didn't seem to matter here, you were judged on who you were, not what you had achieved.

Monday afternoon surpassed even Burnt Cow day. Timothy had become a man - well he had sex for the first time anyway. Shirley had always said she was good with her hands and she proved it yesterday up on the hill, and not just her hands either. He was admittedly infatuated with her sexually but he found he also had affection for her too, which was a bad thing he knew. This was his first experience and was well aware that it wasn't one that was designed to last and he didn't want to make a fool of himself. It was fun and best left at that.

He was also aware it was Tuesday and he'd been here over a week now and had nothing to show for it. The department expected results and he had gone past what would be considered 'a reasonable amount of time'. He had to finish up and leave, having no reasonable cause to be there anymore and the longer he left it, the worse it would become, he could even lose his job.

'Not planning on shooting anyone with that, are you Mr. Montague?'

'Hello Mr. Roystone, you're quite safe, I'd forgotten you were a birdwatcher like myself.'

'Ornithologist.' corrected Roystone, with a smile.

'Sorry - it's for rabbits, the landlord asked me to bag a couple while I was out.'

'Mind if I join you? you are off up the hill I imagine?'

'Yes, of course, I'd be delighted.' replied Timothy.

Timothy and William spent a good morning together, thankfully for Timothy, William Roystone didn't ask any awkward questions, in fact he learnt a great deal from him including how to shoot and gut rabbits, for which Timothy was extremely grateful.

Lunch time and they both brought out packets of Clifford's speciality sandwiches, doorsteps stuffed with rare beef and mustard. Both poured half their beer away discreetly. The view from the hill was spectacular, with exceptional all-round visibility.

'What do you make of that Smallpott chap that came in the bar the other evening?' asked Timothy, casually.

'The rather rotund little chap with the greased back hair, highly polished shoes, gold tiepin and expensive silk shirt? . . . can't say I noticed him much, why do you ask?'

'He stands to inherit that large house down there.' said Timothy, matter-of-factly.

'Oh yes, I think I heard someone in the bar mention it the other day, he owns a hotel on the coast I believe, plans to turn the estate into another more exclusive one.'

Timothy was agog, Roystone had only been here a couple of days and already he knew more than he did after a week. It also explained the villager's interest in having Smallpott bumped off but he kept that to himself.

William Roystone liked Timothy. He wasn't particularly smart but his mind wasn't blinkered either and he picked things up easily. He had narrowed him down to some sort of undercover investigator, obviously new but not free-lance, this ruled out newspapers. He wasn't targeting one person either, this also ruled out private detective. Timothy was looking for something more solid and his interest in the old still in the woods suggested perhaps a government body, possibly Inland Revenue or customs. His choice of cover was excellent of course, and best suited for the situation but his clothes were too new and lacked that worn-in look that brought credibility with it. He could just ask him but that would spoil the fun.

The next few days passed without event. Timothy only bumped into Roystone one more time outside, he seemed to get up early and come back late, stopping only for a short chat and a pint. He himself, decided to spend a second full week in the village, not that he would discover anything but in the hope of gaining some more sexual experience with Shirley. He wasn't disappointed. There was also the lure of the upcoming enquiry that would decide the fate of the Major and the estate. It was taking place on Saturday at the inn itself. That day would be his last in the village and probably in Customs and excise too.

Chapter 16: The Great Gathering

Magnus Makepeace was in his element. It was a rare thing for him to be centre-stage at such a gathering. The legal career he had embarked on, had in its early days, held visions of high drama in court, heading public inquires and perhaps, reaching the lofty heights of himself one day, being addressed as 'My Lord.' It was never to be. The county solicitor's grandiose dreams are just that, dreams, they would never reach fruition when life brings nothing but land disputes, boundary arguments, wills and oaths. He intended to make the most of this enquiry as possible, with the help of his new and allegedly foolproof 'Smith & Winterton Gentleman's Elasticated Rubber Cuffed Preventor,' - guaranteed undergarment for the retention and absorption of seepage. Today he mused, would be a good day.

The Major, the Duke of Stonely, thought otherwise. He sat watching the gathering with some trepidation. The overall feeling was more akin to a coroner's court than a public meeting, on which his future rested so precariously. Perhaps that wasn't the right word, waiting for the nudge into the precipice would have been more appropriate.

The Major had elected for the event to be held in the Stonely Arms Inn. Makepeace hadn't been keen on this at all and insisted that it was held in surroundings that had a more conducive nature to its importance, such as the Town Hall in nearby Stoneleigh. Makepeace had reminded him that although it was neither a public inquiry nor an official hearing, it was still an open court - for want of a better word - and therefore, an allowance had to be made for the attendance of interested parties. The Major pointed out that the inn had played an important part in the life of the estate and that it was in fact the original Court Leet in the late middle ages. Thankfully, Makepeace was a traditionalist and was won round with history. The Major was also aware that because anyone could attend such an open meeting, keeping it isolated to what he considered a controlled environment, suited him better. Yes, the local villagers could and would attend but it was better that than in some town where the press and public had free rein. The other option of holding it in the great Hall on the estate hadn't sat comfortably. The thought of Smallpott taking visual inventory before him, made his skin crawl and was quickly dismissed.

Makepeace had been positioned at the far end of the long bar at a table that had been especially raised to give him an air of authority, oddly

Clifford hadn't seen fit to supply a chair of equal proportions, so when Magnus Makepeace sat down, only his head and shoulders were visible. A small fire had also been lit behind it, despite the warmth of the summer's day. Clifford had been following instructions.

It was half past ten when the Major sat down at the window seat just to the side of Makepeace's position, the seat usually favoured by Timothy. It afforded him a good view down the bar but removed him from centre stage.

The enquiry, as it had become known, was due to start at 11 o'clock, the Major had been there since nine that morning enjoying a condemned man's hearty breakfast. He was keen to be in position before proceedings commenced, rather than walk into a crowded room where all eyes would be on him, he had always shunned the limelight. He was also irked that the so-called private detective had failed to make an appearance and hope against hope, save the day. It happened in books.

Timothy wandered down to the bar at a quarter to 11 to have a last beer, having already packed his bags and stowed them in his little car. Today wasn't going to be a good day. Shirley served him his pint and kept conversation down to little more than a whisper.

'I'll be sad to see you go, Timothy.' she said, putting her hand on his.

'Come to watch the lamb being led to the slaughter then Timmy?' interrupted Clifford.

'No no, not at all' he replied.

'Don't worry old mate, you won't be the only one by a long chalk.'

'What happens to you if Mr Smallpott inherits?' asked Timothy.

'The shit hits the windmill I suppose. Technically the estate owns the village and this Smallpott character will probably turn the Hall into some sort of bloody hotel and pleasure park, we'll lose everything we've all worked for, there'll be a proper road next, it's not right, not natural.' There was genuine remorse in his voice and Timothy knew he spoke for everyone.

In the next ten minutes, the bar started to fill out but not in the normal way. The villagers stayed very much at the entrance end of the bar, each one notably avoiding little more than the occasional glance down the rest of the room. They all pretended that nothing out of the ordinary was happening and had all popped in for a pint at the same time. A long table had been placed down the centre for the main players; a clear dividing line had been invisibly drawn.

Dennis Henderson had taken up position on the right hand side nearest where the Major was currently ensconced. The Major himself however, remained firmly in place. Next to arrive was Hoghorn. The Major took particular pleasure in her presence - to his knowledge and that of the village - this would be the first time she had set foot in the building. She placed herself on the left side of the table, opposite Henderson. The streaming sunlight from the window gave her an ethereal look which was accentuated by her high-necked, black Victorian attire she always wore. Her hair was as always in a tight bun, pulling her face into a severe look with a high forehead. Her hands placed hidden from sight on her lap in a formal manner.

Clifford, not one to miss an opportunity, quietly offered each a drink as they arrived. In Hoghorn's case, a small glass of lemonade, the same was offered to Makepeace. He would have preferred a good whisky but the occasion denied him that option, although a hip flask rested in his case for medical reasons of course. Henderson and the Major had a pint each.

The clock struck eleven. As the last note died away, Makepeace struck the table with a gavel he'd purchased especially for the occasion. He loved the drama.

So did Smallpott, who had timed his entrance exactly as the room fell silent for Makepeace's opening gambit. All eyes fell on him as he opened the door and waddled over to the table. Everyone watched with interest to see which side he'd sit, Henderson or Hoghorn?

If it were possible to get a sound that was quieter than silence itself, it would have been heard then, as Smallpott moved a chair to the head of the table instead. Here, flanked by Henderson and Hoghorn in front, he looked directly at Makepeace and uttered the single word . . . 'proceed.'

This irritated Makepeace greatly. Despite his position of neutrality, he loathed Smallpott. Makepeace needed to re-establish his command and picked up his glass of lemonade and drained it slowly, making everyone wait for him. It was a small token-effort but to him, a valuable one.

'Your Grace, ladies and gentlemen, we are assembled here today,' opened Makepeace avoiding the word 'gathered' when he realised it sounded too much like a wedding.

'To open an enquiry into the unusual will of the Duchess of Stonely, who died five years ago today. As I'm sure most of you are aware by now, a clause stipulated that the estate and hall consisting of . . .'

Makepeace then listed in full detail each and every item, goods and chattels, land and income, leases and rents, loans and bequests that made the Stonely family what it was today.

In the meantime, Shirley discreetly refilled the glasses of Hoghorn and Makepeace with lemonade and sherry for Smallpott. The Major declined. The gentle heat of the fire, combined with the initial boredom as Makepeace droned on, was money in Clifford's pocket, not that he would be charging the 'court' anything, it was the audience it brought with it that was lining his coffers and the party was just about to begin.

Following the Majors discrete instructions, a little kick had been added to the drinks, The Major had intended to go out with a bang. He knew he'd lost but just perhaps if he could turn the whole thing into a shambles, the sentencing could be delayed for a while, and besides, the thought of Hoghorn drinking alcohol was delicious and maybe Smallpott would drop his bloody holier-than-thou pretence.

He had thought of beating a confession out of him, forcing him to declare that he had steered his mother into altering the will in his favour but knew that evidence made under duress was inadmissible and the tables would quickly be turned back on to himself.

'. . . and village fountain.' finished Makepeace taking another sip from his glass. He glanced at his pocket watch he'd placed on the table earlier. It read 11:20, another ten minutes explaining the will, twenty minutes listening to any evidence offered by the Duke to support his case and then break for lunch. In the afternoon, he'd sum up and award the estate. The smell of roast lamb was already penetrating the bar.

'And so the heir to the estate would normally fall to the only child of Lady Stonely, the current Duke,' Makepeace paused and did a curt nod in the Majors direction, all part of the theatrics. 'But Lady Stonely, a magnificent woman by the way, has for reasons best known only to herself, instead instructed that only a grandchild could inherit outright, this offspring being the fruits of the loins of His Grace, the Duke here.'

The phrase that would normally have made Makepeace wince, instead brought a smile, in fact he was stifling a girl-like giggle and reached for the lemonade, which he had noted, seemed curiously bottomless. He also wondered why he had added 'magnificent woman' and hoped nobody noticed his personal interjection. Clearing his throat, he continued.

'In the event of no such issue,' Makepeace paused here and addressed the villagers at the back mouthing the word 'Grandchild' for clarity, 'then the estate as listed previously, shall pass to one Mr. Reginald Smallpott to do with as he wishes.'

Smallpott remained motionless, no expression crossed his face. He just sipped his sherry and looked straight ahead.

'What 'appens to the Major then?' came a voice from the back.

'That Sir, is none of your business.' would normally have been Makepeace's rebuff but he was enjoying himself and welcomed this intrusion as an excuse to display his solicitors art. He glanced at his watch, almost lunchtime, he hoped there'd be roast potatoes and parsnips with the lamb and made a mental note to have the watch glass polished as it seemed to have gone out of focus somewhat.

'The Major would, in this event, retain the use of gatehouse cottage number one and receive a small annuity to supplement his military pension.'

'I aint calling 'im Duke', piped up another voice from the back.

'Mr Smallpott is not entitled to that particular title.' answered Makepeace with some relish and added 'thankfully' a little louder than he intended. . .

. . . 'although, he can use the title Squire if he so desires.' and wished he'd never said it.

Smallpott's seating position came to the fore now. Having his back to the villagers, meant they couldn't judge if their comments were getting to him, which was their intention, no one really hid the fact that he wasn't welcome. Had they seen his face, they might have just noticed an occasional tick in the corner of his eye. Other than that, he retained a painted face.

All Smallpott needed was patience. He could sit the whole thing out without saying a word, in fact he'd be all the better for it.

'I think we'll break for lunch as this juncture' said Makepeace rather surprisingly. The lamb had been getting to him. 'Resume at 1:30 sharp.'

Now this was a turn up, thought the Major, he wasn't alone. Clifford smiled to himself, he couldn't have asked for a better end to the morning and asked Makepeace if he preferred to dine away from the other guests, him being a legal person and all. Magnus Makepeace welcomed this opportunity for some privacy; he'd be able to check on his gentleman's undergarment, which so far, had lived up to its promise.

Shirley escorted him up the stairs to Timothy's now-vacant room. She wasn't sure if it was the stairs creaking or old Makepeace. Having been shown in, Shirley said she'd bring his dinner up immediately.

'Thank you young lady, magnificent breasts.' he said, as she departed. It looked like the special lemonade was working.

'How's the old fart?' asked Clifford, when she returned from taking his dinner up where he had been thanking God for giving her a shapely arse.

'His joints are stiff but his tongue's loosened up' she laughed. 'What about Hoghorn?' she asked.

'Nothing. Not a sausage, she's gone home for lunch thankfully, she'll need more work.

'and Shitface, I mean Smallpott?'

'Same, those two are made of bloody stone I tell you.' finished Clifford, somewhat disappointed. It would only make him redouble his efforts.

The Major, on the other hand, was summing up the morning with Henderson in a corner of the bar, enjoying some of Clifford's warm door-step, roast lamb sandwiches.

'So what are we using to spike their drinks with then?' asked the Major.

'Marie Celeste, the clear stuff.' answered Henderson with a grin

'Oh can't say I remember that one, good is it?'

'Oh yes, effects people in different ways. Clifford and I did an experiment one evening a couple of years ago in here, Alf Hicks the mute wouldn't stop talking, Mrs Cooper had it off with her husband and his brother in the smoke house around the back, and Johns the Jones farted a rendition of 'Men of Harlech' until he coughed and covered the piano in diarrhoea.'

'I wondered where that had gone.' laughed the Major.

'No-one wanted to play it anymore.'

'I think Makepeace is becoming affected, he's started saying odd things out loud, rather than in his head, Peter Watkins did that.

'Watkins the Jessie?'

'That's the one, Cliff won't turn his back on him now.'

The break had been a welcome reprieve.

'It's a nappy I tell you', whispered Shirley to Clifford as they stood in the hallway looking though the slight opening of the door at Makepeace who was sound asleep on the bed with his trousers around his thin ankles.

'I thought you were joking. If I hadn't seen it with my own eyes, I wouldn't have believed you.' said Clifford and added that she would have to wake him up.

'What do you mean, me?'

'I'm not going in there, I'd piss myself laughing.'

'Then perhaps he could lend you his spare.' answered Shirley, sarcastically.

Shirley brought the door gently closed, looked at Clifford and then banged on the door loudly, 'Five minutes Mr. Makepeace' and then whispered to Clifford 'Takes a woman don't it.'

A grunt was heard from the other side of the door as Makepeace stirred. Clifford and Shirley hurried down the creaking stairs, carefully walking in-step to sound as one.

Everyone was back in position and chatting when Makepeace returned to the top table. He picked up the gavel and brought it down with some force. Everything went quiet as their attention was now firmly on that of Magnus Makepeace who was still holding the gavel and staring at his now-broken pocket watch in front of him. He continued.

'We have come to the stage in the proceedings, where I must formally ask His Grace, the Major, I mean the Duke of Stonely, if he can produce any proof of a living heir fathered by him, by some means or other.'

'Shagging's the normal way.' said a voice from the back, a little too loudly but it got a cheer from the rest of the villagers.

The Major rose from his position, addressed Makepeace and reluctantly admitted 'I have no known living relatives.'

'Then I see no reason why Mr. Reginald Smallpott . . .'

'I'm his half-brother' interrupted Roystone, who had appeared from the shadows.

'Whose brother?' whispered Timothy to Shirley beside him.

'The Majors, I hope.' said Shirley, suddenly realising the room had gone deathly quiet.

All eyes were on Mr.Roystone as he took centre stage and faced Hoghorn, 'aren't I, mother?'

Two stunned silences in a row was more than most could take in, mouths were hitting the ground at an alarming rate. Everybody had stopped breathing and looked at Hoghorn who just said 'Fuck it.', touched her neck, closed her eyes and toppled over backwards in her chair.

Makepeace had a spasm and dropped down into his chair with enough force to split one of the rubberised gaiters around the leg hole of his Gentleman's Preventor. Henderson smiled inwardly, Smallpott didn't break his statue-like composure. Clifford was already unscrewing the top of a whisky bottle, hoping he had enough tumblers for everyone. Timothy remained unaffected by it all, he hardly knew the people involved so its effect was limited to just amusing. The Major, however, remained staring at Roystone.

Hoghorn was tilted gently back into position and revived with a slice of stilton wafted under her nose; smelling salts were not in great demand in the countryside. A shot of brandy was placed before her, which she downed in one and resumed her more usual countenance, looking fixedly into the middle distance.

Makepeace banged his gavel down and called out as best he could 'Order, Order' in an attempt to silence the rising voices of the villagers at the back of the inn, to no avail.

Peace, of a sort, was restored after a few minutes, enough time for the villagers inside to swell to twice the number. A window at the back had been opened in readiness to pass on the 'courts' proceedings to the gathering crowd that was forming outside.

Clifford was desperate to set up a bar outside but didn't want to miss anything, knowing just how exaggerated it would become when news was second hand.

Back on his feet, Makepeace asked 'Are you informing the court Mr…?'

'Roystone Sir, William Roystone.'

'Mr. Roystone, that your father was the Late Duke Stonely and your mother is Chastity Hoghorn?'

'Yes, that is correct' came the simple reply, it needed nothing more.

'And are you older or younger than the Major here?'

'Younger, Sir.' Makepeace was warming to this stranger, at least he addressed him as Sir, the first to show him any respect.

'And do you have any children?' for the first time there was hope in his voice.

The audience were now on tender hooks, so much had happened in such a short period of time, breath was again being held.

'Sadly, no.' came the reply. A sigh of disappointment filled the room.

'Then as a younger half brother of which the Duchess of Stonely obviously had no knowledge, I have to stick to the spirit of the will as intended if not the word, your intervention, dramatic as it was, has no bearing on the final outcome I'm sorry to say, we have to move on.

There was a feeling of great disappointment amongst almost everyone in the room and those outside, as the news filtered through the window.

'However, I'm dying to know more' added Makepeace with a broad grin on his face. A silent cheer went up, except for those outside who forgot the silent bit. A blood vessel in Smallpott's temple started pulsing rapidly.

'I think Dr Strange is the best one to explain, under the circumstances' said Roystone, moving out of the limelight to be replaced by the aforementioned Doctor himself.

'Am I under oath?' asked the Doctor

'Consider yourself so, Doctor.' replied Makepeace, not that anyone had sworn an oath in the first place, he just wanted him to get on with it.

'The Duke, the Majors father,' he added for clarity, 'came to me one evening, concerned that one of his servants had got herself pregnant, not an unusual situation even these days, and could I do anything about it. I told the Duke I would have to examine the female, to confirm the condition first. The young lady concerned was Chastity Hoghorn, nanny to His Graces son, Rupert. The examination revealed that indeed she was with child, early stages, nothing openly visible. I asked her if the other party involved, a stable lad probably, would be prepared to do the right thing. She laughed and said it was unlikely the culprit would marry her, as his wife, the Duchess, wouldn't agree. I spoke to the Duke later, who confirmed that he had indeed taken advantage of her when he was drunk and was prepared to pay the price to keep both her silence and see that the child was given a home, just not around here. It was an embarrassment he didn't want reminding of.

I was later to learn, that the child had been given to a couple of a suitable background and that its upbringing would be that similar to one that he himself would have provided.

'I thought Doctors swore some oath that prevented them from divulging this sort of thing' said Hoghorn who still remained motionless focusing on nothing.

'Ah yes, how remiss of me, Doctor, I should have made that clear before you offered testimony' said Makepeace.

'Oh, I'm not actually a doctor, I'm a vet.

'And do the good people of the village know this?' asked Makepeace astonished.

'Yes.' was the chorus from the village people.

Timothy hadn't, he'd let the man examine his genitals. He started to feel a little sick.

'This is all very interesting but as I've said before, it has no relevance to the case in-hand' said Makepeace and added in a quieter voice 'I hope the girl with the tits brings me some more lemonade.' Makepeace was still oblivious he was speaking his thoughts out loud.

'I think it may have, Sir,' interrupted Roystone again. 'If I may continue the story?'

'Christ yes.' said Makepeace watching Shirley's approaching bosom.

'My hasty adoption, was of course unofficial, my new parents were of a social standing similar to that of the Stonely's, in fact, they were distant friends. Sadly, the wife - my adoptive mother - produced a male child of a weak nature who scarcely drew breath before it expired. It was perhaps fortuitous that my arrival coincided with this event. A substitution was made and the events forgotten. My adoptive name,' he turned to face Smallpott, 'is Waller-Boyce.'

Reginald Smallpott lifted his glass of sherry to his lips and drained it slowly, he turned even whiter than his pale skin would normally allow. A bead of sweat ran down from his temple but he remained silent.

The hairs on the back of the Majors neck rose and a shudder went through his body.

'Not a Hampshire Waller-Boyce?' said Makepeace who was now totally enthralled with the situation and hadn't noticed he'd wet himself.

'The very same, Sir' answered Roystone or Waller-Boyce who hadn't taken his eyes off Smallpott.

'Well, bugger me' replied Makepeace.

Peter Watkins, the village homosexual, looked over the crowd of villagers from the back at Makepeace and declined the invitation.

The Major was holding his glass in front of his face, conscious that it would cover any facial expression he may be involuntarily giving. He was having trouble in his head. Thoughts were desperately fighting for processing time. William Roystone the private detective he'd employed and never seen, turns out to be his half brother and the infamous Waller-Boyce. Suddenly, the battlefield had been tilted in a totally obscure direction. Everyone in the Army knew of Major Waller-Boyce. So, apparently, did Smallpott, the Major saw the sign.

Waller-Boyce, who now held centre stage, looked over to Stonely 'I imagine that has come as a bit of a shock, Rupert?'

This sudden lack of protocol brought a silence that was starting to become commonplace that day. The Major had been addressed by his first name, the preserve of friends and family, but Waller-Boyce was family, apparently.

'Indeed it has . . .'

'Winston.' added Waller-Boyce.

'Winston.' replied Major Stonely, somewhat embarrassed.

'I myself, was a Major in the Army', Winston Waller-Boyce continued to no-one in particular but turned and rounded once again on Smallpott and added . . . 'in Military Intelligence'

Smallpott flicked a quick glance at Hoghorn.

'In India.'

Smallpott's lips visibly tightened, to those that could see.

'Second Lieutenant, Withers.' added Waller-Boyce, clearly addressing Smallpott.

'Smallpott.' corrected Smallpott.

'No - your real name.'

'As I've just said, Reginald Smallpott.'

'Second Lieutenant Reginald Withers, quartermaster in the British Army in India, stationed in Pongee.

'Hardly.' he smirked.

'Army Deserter.' added Waller-Boyce.

'Utter nonsense.' Smallpott replied dismissively.

'Ran a very successful black market operation in government property.' At this point, Waller-Boyce glanced at Stonely, who was staring at

Smallpott with his eyes wide open and clearly fighting to keep his composure.

'I think you're mistaken, Mr.Waller-Boyce' said Smallpott, looking him directly in the eye for the first time.

'Acting Second Lieutenant Withers, British Army India Division? Deserted the army after having made a fortune on the black market. Took a new identity, not difficult for a man with your connections. Made sure it was that of a reserved occupation, thus avoiding any military links or history. Opened up a hotel on the south coast in Worthing, specialising in the convalescing wealthy, such as the Stonely's and used this cover to import contraband through your black market channels. It was then, that you discovered a talent for ingratiating yourself with soon-to-be widows. In fact, we can't actually be sure what your real name is, you probably don't even remember it yourself.

'Oh for Christ's sake Shirley, said Clifford, 'I'm going to have to start writing this down, I'm getting lost - it is Shirley isn't it?'

Smallpott was determined not to be dragged deeper into this ever-evolving drama, he had not intended to utter a single word during the proceedings other than 'thank you' at the end. He could read Waller-Boyce's plan to discredit him in the eyes of the solicitor and everyone else. Waller-Boyce was clever but he couldn't have any proof that was a certainty, he must remain silent, but then again, an innocent man would naturally defend himself, this was dangerous ground.

'What's the point of this charade, Waller-Boyce, you've lost, you've all lost, trying to discredit me in front of everyone with these fanciful stories makes no difference. The will clearly states, that if no heir is produced, I get the lot. This isn't a trial.' Smallpott looked directly at Makepeace for support and confirmation.

'Well, not strictly true,' said Makepeace, leaning back in his chair and almost disappearing from view behind the table. He leaned forward again quickly.

'This meeting is more akin to a coroner's court, we don't seek to place blame but to establish the facts, identify those concerned and decide if further enquires need be made, It is for me and me alone to decide who gets the stuff.' finished Makepeace, slipping into more down to earth language.

'And this gentleman,' continued Makepeace indicating Waller-Boyce 'has suggested that you may not be the person you purport yourself to be and that you may have a dubious and possibly criminal background that shows an ability to deceive and could therefore have foreseeably brought undue pressure and influence to bear on the Duchess whilst she was in a vulnerable state of mind.'

A cheer rose from the back of the inn from the villagers, Makepeace almost stood up to take a bow, whilst Waller Boyce remained staring at Smallpott regretting he no longer had the authority to don his military uniform for added intimidation. He had never needed to resort to violence, his authority and reputation in the Army, had alone been enough to bring a man down, that and playing with his service revolver but at this moment he was fighting the urge to drag this little man out of his seat, rip off his oh-so-neat jacket and shirt and reveal his crude military tattooed arms he was almost certain Withers would have.

'Any chance of some more tits.' said Makepeace holding up his empty class. With that, the spell was broken, much to Waller-Boyce's regret.

A mutual agreement for a 30 minute break was accepted. Hoghorn and Smallpott left the pub and went off in separate directions, her to the gatehouse and he to Riverside Cottage.

For the Major, it was a welcome break he needed to absorb what he had just heard. If that really was Withers, he had a score to settle and a big one at that. He also appeared to have a half brother to boot, one he didn't welcome at all.

Clifford hastily erected a bench outside, with a barrel of Badgers Bottom to slake the thirst of the many that couldn't get inside the inn.

Waller-Boyce strolled out, sat on the bench in front of the fountain and lit his pipe. Stonely watched from inside. He found himself being pulled in several directions at once, this man, his half-brother, could send him to prison and cost him the estate, if he knew Withers, then he'd know he too, was involved. Waller-Boyce could gaol the two of them.

'You'd best go and talk to your brother.' said Henderson quietly. The Majors mind had been made up, he just needed the push.

'So, bit of a rum do all this' said Stonely as he sat down next to Waller-Boyce outside, he wasn't comfortable with calling him Winston, that would take a while if he had the time.

'Yes indeed, a rum do.' Waller-Boyce took a long pull on his pipe and looked at the inn reflectively; pipes do that to a man, force him into a slower more sedate pace.

'The Waller-Boyces ?' asked Stonely.

'No longer I'm afraid, natural causes, no other children, the estate eaten up by tax duties and bad investments.

'Oh, sorry to hear that, have to admit to not really taking much of an interest in family and friends. What did you do?' asked the Major.

'Spent my entire life in the Army, they were my real family I suppose,' carried on Waller-Boyce, 'nurtured, fed and watered, that was all I needed until I retired and then I had to fend for myself, got bored, took up bird watching and the odd private investigation.'

'Yes, I was going to ask about that.' smiled the Major weakly and wished he hadn't.

'Interesting case, I thought at the time,' continued Waller-Boyce. 'Transparent of course but Smallpott's gain was far in excess of the usual widow's bequest, I mean it's tantamount to inheriting a whole village.'

'Had you been born on the right side of the blanket, you'd be Lord of the village with me.' added the Major.

'Sadly, born a bastard.' replied Waller-Boyce with a smile.

The Major knew that hadn't helped. The irony of hiring a private detective to dig the dirt on Smallpott only to reveal that the detective was a man he had taken great care to deceive in the past. Waller-Boyce must be aware of Stonely's part in setting up the black market in India. A thought struck the Major like a hammer, Waller-Boyce could end up with the estate!

'How much did Withers take from you?' asked Waller-Boyce casually.

'£51,000' replied Stonely without a pause, he knew.

'A tidy sum.'

'You know the whole thing, don't you?' asked Stonely.

'Oh yes.' nodded Waller-Boyce turning over the silver plated lighter in his hand.

'I used to call you 'the broom' said Waller-Boyce.

'The Broom?'

'Never left anything behind, all tracks covered in paperwork, I admired the organisation of the operation, military precision, your name came up as a possible contender occasionally but you were careful not to appear whiter than white, small overlooked indiscretions here and there, the odd case of whisky turning up at the officers club, all unofficially acceptable, you never fitted the profile I was looking for.'

'Withers, on the other hand, did but he had a cunning nature, he learnt by each mistake and got smarter, in the end I recommended he was sent to Pongee. A dead-end surplus camp in the middle of nowhere, lots of redundant equipment and nowhere to unload it. I made a mistake there. That's where I think you discovered him?'

'Yes, quite by accident. Didn't know Pongee existed until I needed some spare parts for some historic regimental display and discovered this depot. I never actually met or spoke to Withers, everything was done through a trusted middle-man, no names, no pack-drill sort of thing, anyway, Withers had somehow found an outlet and so I started to write off equipment and send it in his direction. It was ideal, this was stuff that no one wanted but we couldn't give it away for obvious reasons and so I absorbed him into my little group. The income was turned into shares through a broker, all Withers' idea, easy to hide and transfer, no cash, no questions. I trusted the little bastard.'

'When did you discover there was no money?'

About a month ago, I'd gone up to London after arranging my shares to be cashed in and the money put in a safety deposit box. It was then I discovered they'd been swapped for worthless ones in 'Spanish Amalgamated Lemons.'

A wide smile crossed Waller-Boyces' face. He then asked, 'What happened in Pongee when you visited?'

He wasn't there - rather annoyingly; I had been looking forward to meeting him in the guise of the auditor. I signed off the inspection as correct at the time, I didn't want to arouse suspicions. In fact, that's when I started to shut the whole thing down, everyone had done well out of it and some cashed in their shares early, I had no suspicion of anything untoward then. It was ironic that it was your office that employed me to examine the paper work and uncover the source behind it all. Good thing we never met, I imagine. I had made a lot of money out of it and the last thing I wanted to do was draw attention to myself. It was to be my pension if I needed it. I stayed on for another five years until mother died, then I left and went home.

'You didn't actually need the money did you, at the time?'

'No, as you can see, I come from a wealthy family, I fully expected to take over the estate and enjoy my retirement, but as you know, that wasn't to be and now I could lose the lot and no special pension to fall back on. A lesson learnt, perhaps.

Stonely hung his head low for a moment, he'd just admitted to Waller-Boyce who he was, it was almost like a confessional but the consequences could be dire. It's just that he was such a likable chap and easy to talk to.

Waller-Boyce leant back on the bench and watched Smallpott approaching the inn, it was obvious he wasn't pleased to see them sat together.

Another 10 minutes later and the meeting would be re-opened with Makepeace taking up position. He had spent the last 20 minutes chatting rather loudly with Clifford, whilst the endowed Shirley, topped up his lemonade.

'I don't know why I don't come here more often, your soft furnishings are delightful.' said Makepeace, hardly taking his eyes off Shirley's breasts, which were now playing an important part in his life. He had felt a stirring in an area where no stirrings had been since his wedding night all those years ago. His first and only permitted forage into the world of carnal knowledge, had sadly, been misguided and short-lived. He had accidentally entered, what his new wife referred to in the heated argument that followed as the 'tradesman's entrance', despite his assurance that it was purely down to inexperience and misinterpretation of the landmarks in the dark and his further insistence that he had mistaken her moans for that of pleasure not pain did little to appease his bride, who appeared to have a better anatomical knowledge than he had given her credit for, certainly better than his.

From then on, it had been a marriage of convenience, convenient for her, bloody inconvenient for him, certain in the knowledge that one slip of the tongue, metaphorically speaking, would again land him in the shit, especially as he'd just become a young partner in a solicitors firm of some standing, locally.

Fortunately, she died a couple of years later. Not for her of course, or the coal merchant who was on top of her at the time or even the farmer who ran over them with his tractor in the field. It was said, the expression on her face was akin to that of pure ecstasy, less so for the coalman whose testicles had burst in the last thrust of his life being forcibly pressed home with the weight of a Ferguson-Brown Type A tractor tyre.

Makepeace had received a lot of sympathy but not of a physical nature sadly but he couldn't help smiling at the sound of a passing tractor. He carried on a celibate life, not through choice but as time wore on, his body lost the capacity to retain liquids for any length of time, something that hindered any physical relationship and brought him into the world of mail-order rubberised undergarments.

'Shouldn't you be getting up, Mr.Makepeace?' said Shirley.

'Well I'm game if you are, my dear.'

'The table.'

'I say, you're very bold.'

'I mean the meeting table.'

'What, oh yes, of course, silly me, the meeting.'

Chapter 17: Bottoms Up

Suitably rested, Makepeace banged his gavel with fresh enthusiasm and restrained himself from saying 'On Your marks, get set . . .' and continued.

'It would appear that Mr.Roystone, or Waller-Boyce, has cast serious doubt as to who . . ' there was a pause whilst Makepeace focused on Smallpott and narrowed his eyes in an effort to remember what his name was, he eventually settled for '. . . he really is.'

Smallpott remained motionless, stolidly starring at Makepeace, the whole thing was turning into a farce.

'Has anyone else got any last minute revelations they'd like to expose?'

'I have an announcement.' said Timothy, taking a step forward. 'I work for His Majesties Custom and Excise.' There was no response.

'We all knew that, love' said Shirley reaching across the bar and touching his arm with her finger tips, the way women do.

'When?'

'Last Wednesday.'

'Oh.' said Timothy, somewhat crestfallen.

Smallpott broke the silence. 'Whilst we're on the subject of who's who, how do we know that the Duke is who he says he is?, he's been away since he was little-more than a child and as for Waller-Boyce, well how convenient he should appear on the scene as the long-lost half-brother and son of a servant who couldn't possibly recognise her own child since he was little more than a babe in arms at the time. Oh yes, Waller-Boyce is a clever man, clever enough to concoct this whole charade being played out before you, he'll try to win you over with charm and drama, and what's the point, what is it all about, an heir to the Stonely estate, of which, there clearly is none.

Smallpott had reached his crescendo and stopped for breath; he had held the attention of the masses and planted the seed of doubt.

There was silence as it dawned on people that they had taken it for granted that the Major was indeed the real Duke of Stonely. For the first time, even Henderson stopped to consider the idea but just as quickly dismissed it. The Major and he shared history.

'A valid point indeed.' agreed Makepeace, who was having trouble remembering who was who anyway.

'The birthmark would prove it.' offered Dr Strange.

'Care to elaborate on that, Doctor?' asked Makepeace.

'The old Duke and his son, both shared a birthmark, something I myself had witnessed, I believe it ran in the Stonely family. If Major Stonely is the boy I knew as Rupert, son of the Duke, he will still bear that mark, and so, I would imagine, would Mr.Waller-Boyce, although perhaps not as defined as the original, considering the circumstances.

'Why are we looking at birthmarks for pity's sake?' interrupted Smallpott, 'It has no relevance to the outcome of the inheritance.'

Makepeace chose to ignore him, this was far more interesting. 'And what form does this birthmark take?' he asked.

'A mark or blemish that resembles the shape of Italy.'

'And where is this?' Makepeace enquired.

'In the Mediterranean.' answered the doctor.

'No no, I mean the position of the birthmark.'

'Oh that, it's on the back of the scrotum.'

'I see,' said Makepeace, 'and you say this is a family trait?'

'Yes, dating back to first Duke himself, I'm given to understand.'

'Are there any portraits of family members with their tackle out?' said Makepeace speaking his thoughts out loud to sounds of suppressed laughter from the back of the room.

'None to my knowledge.' answered Doctor Strange, bemused by the question.

'Would you be prepared to prove this, if required?' asked Makepeace, addressing the Major directly.

The massed villagers leaned slightly forward as one, it's not often the gentry's genitals were discussed so openly.

'Bit of a sore point, I'm afraid,' said the Major, who had suffered many emotions during this inquest but hadn't figured on embarrassment being one of them.

'I suffered a wounding during my service in India, which resulted in a minor operation. I fear that scar tissue may have covered up the evidence.' The villagers, to a man, started whistling Colonel Bogey.

'Silence, please.' said Makepeace, when he finally worked out the connection.

'I can confirm that he had a birthmark there', added Henderson.
A hush fell over the villagers.

'We used to swim in the lake sometimes as kids, naked, you can't help but notice those sorts of things.' finished Henderson, blushing. Peter Watkins made a mental note to get to know Denis Henderson better.

'Me too,' came a female voice from the back. 'he hid my knickers.'

'Doreen' said the Major and Henderson in unison.

Makepeace's attention shifted to the voice at the back of the room. 'And you witnessed this mark, I take it?' he asked.

'Well sort of. The water was a bit chilly back then and it looked more like the Isle of Wight to me.'

Laughter broke out from everyone except Doreen's husband, who just stood there opened mouth.

'And have you seen this mark since?'

'Chance would be a fine thing.' She laughed.

'That's a no then, I take it.' said Makepeace, with a little bit of disappointment in his voice, he had spotted who he presumed to be Doreen's husband standing behind her. He wasn't a picture of happiness.

'And have you two been swimming recently, Mr Henderson?'

'No, Sir.' he had to admit.

Makepeace turned to face Waller-Boyce, 'So Mr Waller-Boyce, do you also have this mark?'

'I'm not sure I've ever been in a position to observe.'

A murmur of amusement arose in the background.

'Drop your trousers.' shouted a voice from the back.

'Would you be prepared to suffer the indignation of a physical inspection? it would save a considerable amount of time.' asked Makepeace.

For the first time in his life, Waller-Boyce felt awkward, it was a new emotion for him. He nodded in agreement. A cheer came from the villagers, who expected a show. Makepeace turned his attention to the Major who followed Waller-Boyce's lead and also nodded. A second, louder cheer followed.

'I suggest we take a break, whilst evidence-gathering is put . . . in hand.' said Makepeace, priding himself on the quip, no one cheered. 'I will also require two, male volunteers to act as witnesses.'

Clifford found something better to do, as Makepeace looked around the room for suitable candidates for the unpleasant task.

As the arrangements were being made, the Major and Waller-Boyce went upstairs to ready themselves for 'small arms inspection', as someone had shouted out earlier, playing on the joint military connection. Meantime, some of the male villagers had formed a queue for the toilet. A voice at the front was heard to ask Doreen to "hold the bloody mirror still." It wasn't that of her husband. Outside, news of the event had filtered through to the gathered crowd. The less-inhibited farmers gathered around the two cars parked outside the inn where their wing mirrors had been twisted into unfamiliar positions. Many of the village ladies had gathered together in the baker's tea shop across the square, keen not to appear overly interested in the recent goings on. Now they were being entertained to a sight of bear-arsed husbands and farmhands, attempting to cock their legs in the air, a task made harder with their trousers around their ankles.

'Is it Morris dancing?' asked one, another voiced an opinion of pagan origin.

'That's your Arthur isn't it? No wonder you always look tired.'

'He can plough my furrow anytime.' giggled another.

'I'd have thought John Thomas would have had a little more.'

'He makes up for it with his hands.' came a voice from the sweet trolley.

Shirley emerged from the kitchen, oblivious of the recent turn of events and got behind the bar just in time to hear Makepeace finishing off a sentence . . .

' . . . both the Major and Mr. Waller-Boyce share a birthmark in the shape of Italy on the scrotum.'

'Timothy's got one of those, only it's on his bollocks.' said Shirley to Clifford.

The inn went silent. She looked up, to find everyone was staring at her. Clifford leaned over and whispered in her ear.

'Oh I didn't know that, you live and learn don't you.'

Timothy crossed his legs and turned bright red, as did Shirley when she realised the implication. There was a delayed cheer from outside and shouts of 'Well done, Timmy.' A weak smile crossed his face and he glanced at Shirley, who had her hand across her mouth.

'Any more?' called out Makepeace.

'I've got a third nipple, does that count?' came a voice from the crowd. 'No, you're just odd' said Makepeace and continued. 'Timothy, I gather?' he said looking directly at him. Timothy swallowed, he knew what was coming. 'We're reliably informed,' Makepeace threw a glance at Shirley who giggled, 'that you also carry this particular distinguishing feature, is this correct?'

'I've not seen it personally, Sir.'

'I imagine not, one would have to be in the enviable position of extreme flexibility to gain such intimate knowledge,' Makepeace's eyes glazed over for a moment as he carried that thought several stages further. Snapping back to the present, he pressed on 'Who is your father?'

'I never knew my father, sir, he died before I was born.'

'But you know his name.'

'No sir.'

'I take it, he wasn't married to your mother?'

'No sir, My mother had always told me it was an officer who was sent abroad at short notice, on a secret mission and he never returned, presumed killed in action.'

'And your mother never knew his name?'

'She always referred to him as "Your father", Sir.'

'Naturally, as one would. Your mother, is she still alive?'

'No, sir.'

'Where were you born?'

'In a village just outside Bovington, Sir. Close to the army base.'

Most people had already put two and two together, the thought that his mother may have had several male friends just never occurred to Timothy and those that knew him didn't want to spoil his memory of his mother. Strangely, the villagers felt the same, an affection of sorts had grown up around him.

'Pity, and I don't suppose you have anything that belonged to your father at all, a memento perhaps?'

Timothy brightened up, 'Yes I do.'

'And do you have it here at all?'

'Yes.'

'Perhaps, if it's convenient, you could show us?'

'Sorry, yes of course.' Timothy left the bar and went outside to his car to much cheering from the gathered crowd. He was embarrassed but felt a little bit like a film star. He returned and placed a package in front of Makepeace and stepped back. With caution Makepeace unfolded the brown, waxed paper and revealed a hand gun.

'This was your fathers?'

'So my mother assured me, yes.' said Timothy.

'Mr Waller-Boyce, perhaps you would be good enough to examine the item, having been in military intelligence, you would be the most qualified.'

Makepeace had thought about asking the Duke but he'd probably shoot Smallpott with it. He didn't know Waller-Boyce held the same compulsion.

'With the deftness of a man used to handling firearms, Waller-Boyce flicked back a catch and allowed the cylinder to hinge forward, exposing five full chambers and one empty one. He removed the rounds and continued to examine the weapon carefully.

'Its not military issue' he said, finally.

'Not a service revolver from a military man then?' suggested Makepeace.

'Not necessarily, it's not uncommon for officers to buy their own pistols or be given their fathers if they had a military background, almost a right of passage, as it were. The pistol does not have a Military issue stamp on the metal but it does have an engraving, a shield and banner but it's far too worn to identify the original owner.' Waller-Boyce looked down the barrel of the empty pistol directly at Smallpott and snapped it shut with an oily click, turned and handed it back to Makepeace.

The whole operation had been carried out in near-silence except for the murmur of voices carrying out a step by step report along a chain of people outside. By the time it reached the Tea Shop, it had been translated as: Makepeace was holding the Major's penis, instead of pistol.

'I've done that' said Rosie Leigh. All the women turned to look at her. 'It was his birthday.' She smiled.

'Well, I hope you've washed your hands.' The tea room erupted into laughter.

Dismissing the gun as invalid evidence, it left the burden of proof in Timothy's trousers and everybody had already worked that out. With reluctance, Timothy headed upstairs to the accompaniment of a slow hand clap and the two witnesses. He had thought of asking Dr Strange to give a statement, as it was he who had previously assisted in the removal of the sheep ticks around, what his mother used to call, his 'love eggs and sausage' but the doctors well-practiced hands had worked independently of his eyes. He knew he'd still end up touching his toes.

Clifford took the opportunity to refresh glasses as Makepeace called for a fifteen minute recess; he had more pressing things on his mind. His Gentleman's Preventor had, by now, become quite sodden, the absorbent lambs wool padding in the rubber cuffs was at its limits and with his back to the fire, it had become his own personal Turkish steam bath. He feared his own testicles were now par-boiled and probably lobster red.

The Major sat outside on the fountain bench as before, waiting to see of Waller-Boyce would join him. After a couple of minutes, he arrived. They sat and watched Smallpott stroll a little way down the lane, smoking a thin cigar. Hoghorn had glided off to the gatehouse, as expected.

Both the Major and Waller-Boyce had served at bases along the south coast as trainee officers and both had taken advantage of the 'facilities' offered there off-barracks.

'Timothy, yours or mine?' asked Waller-Boyce quietly.

'Could be either.' answered the Major.

'Best if he were yours you'd get the estate then, well he would but I'm sure as his father, he wouldn't kick you out now, besides I see a problem I think Smallpott might try to exploit.'

'What about that pistol? it wasn't mine.' said the Major.

'Nor mine, in fact if that crest had been readable it could have removed young Timothy from the playing field, thank God he had the balls.' They both smiled.

The quiet was broken by a scream from the blacksmiths behind the hardware store. Jethro Tutter was applying to be the village idiot.

He had carefully twisted some bailing wire into the shape of Italy and had heated it up in the still-hot forge. Securely clamped in a vice and glowing a dull red, he had slowly backed towards it with his trousers off and his cheeks parted.

He was found, wedged in a wooden bucket, crying. A crowd had gathered and much effort was expended trying to remove the bucket that seemed to be held on by vacuum alone. A hefty clout with a mallet broke the base and the wooden staves fell apart, revealing Jethro's cherry-red buttocks.

'You idiot.' laughed the blacksmith, Jethro had branded the word 'Italy' backwards on one of his buttocks.

Chapter 18: Win Some, Lose Some

With Jethro's incident still fresh in their minds, the meeting re-assembled as before. Makepeace had spent his time locked in a room, naked from the waist down, trying to wring out his Gentlemans Preventor in the sink. His lower trunk showed the obvious signs of having been immersed in water for far too long and skin pruning was evident. It had done little to improve what little he had been blessed with. With some effort and almost a whole tub of talcum powder, Makepeace had eased on the now cold, damp and heavy garment back in place, utilising his braces to hold it up. Legal pink ribbon had been tied around the rubberised leg gaiters for added security.

Makepeace settled back into the chair, for hopefully the last time. The assembled crowd waited patiently. What should have only have been a couple of hours, had taken most of the day and physical weariness was setting in. He banged his gavel down to signal the last act in this drawn out but utterly fascinating play.

'It would appear that Master Timothy here, has indeed been geographically approved.' said Makepeace with a broad grin.

A thunderous cheer rattled the copper bed warming pans nailed to the walls. Shirley jumped up and down in delight and many others were more than pleased she was so actively enjoying the moment.

'I think we are, at last, nearing the end of our quest. I am happy that the Major is, in fact, the true Duke of Stonely and Mr.Waller-Boyce is his half-brother. I am also happy that Timothy is indeed the offspring of the Major . . . or his half-brother.'

'Bastard.' said Smallpott calmly.

'I must inform you, Mr. Smallpott, that sort of language isn't welcome in these premises.' completely forgetting they were gathered in the village pub.

'Bastard, in the legal sense of illegitimate, Mr. Makepeace,' continued Smallpott, 'I think you'll find that a bastard has no right of inheritance.'

'You are of course quite right, Mr. Smallpott, in the event of a death, only the legitimate heirs can inherit . . . had the Duchess died without making a will. However she did and she can leave what she wants to whom she likes, yourself being an example. It is clear to any legal mind that the intended benefactor be a Stonely blood relation, one generation removed, a position Mr. Timothy Montague fits precisely. There is a certain problem with clarity as to the exact parentage of Timothy, with respect to the Major or Mr. Waller-Boyce, the latter being the illegitimate offspring of the Duke but a blood relation of the male linage in the eyes of the law nonetheless, if perhaps somewhat diluted.'

The audience were impressed, they didn't understand but the tone implied Smallpott was wrong, which was fine with them.

'The Duchess of Stonely,' carried on Makepeace, 'expressed a desire that the estate, wherever possible, should remain in the hands of a Stonely, although it was evident that she didn't have much faith in her son, the present Duke. I do believe that this may have been different if she had knowledge of a second son, Mr. Waller-Boyce, although not of her loins, he was still a Stonely by blood and has led an exemplary career within the armed forces, something I think the old Duke would have been proud of.'

Makepeace was in his element now, he had the full and complete attention of everyone. Little did he realise, that most were enthralled with the small puffs of white powder that appeared to be emanating from the back of Makepeace's chair as he rocked backwards and forwards in his oration. Each one was caught in the heat of the fire behind him and sparkled like sprinkled iron filings, accompanied with a gentle phutt sound.

'The alternative of awarding the estate to yourself, Mr. Smallpott, has caused me to have some considerable doubt as to your true identity and the influence that may have been put upon the Duchess in her latter years. The final decision has rested with me now for some time and it has weighed heavy. The will is quite clear and formal but its intent was even clearer. The value of the estate is not one that is measured in monetary terms, but that of heritage and tradition. The Duchess would have been keen to keep the status quo of the estate and village intact, something I fear is not of interest to you, Mr. Smallpott.

'Get on with it, for Christ's sake.' came a voice from a dark corner at the back, it sounded a little like Clifford's.

'However,' resumed Makepeace, 'because of the uncertainty and complications of the exact Stonely bloodline, I find I can not award the estate to Mr. Timothy Montague outright.

There was a shape intake of breath that almost removed all the oxygen from the room.

'I therefore, have decided to instead divide the entire estate between the Duke, Mr. Waller-Boyce and Mr. Timothy Montague evenly, as I'm sure each will keep the other in check.

The cheer resounded around the village square like no other. The women in the tea rooms clapped their hands together, now there was work to be done, for tonight would see a party like no other and there were cakes to be baked.

Timothy was nonplussed, he'd come from nothing and now owned a third of a stately home. Waller-Boyce liked the decision because it was a sensible one but was shocked that he had become part of it.

The Major liked it because he still had a home and Smallpott had been trounced. The thought of sharing it with Waller-Boyce was no hardship, he was starting to like the man. Timothy however was an unknown quantity but he seemed a likeable, if somewhat naïve, chap. He could be moulded and had two of the best mentors he could ever wish for.

Smallpott remained seated, unlike Makepeace, who stood up and was greeted with an enthusiastic round of applause, he opened his arms in a wide embrace and felt his braces twang free. He sat down quickly, releasing a jet of talcum powder from the back of the Gentleman's Preventor, that ignited instantly, shattered the chair, blowing his clothes clean off, leaving him naked, except for two pink ribbons around his thighs and what looked like a garter belt around his waist. A wad of sodden lambs wool smacked Smallpott in the face, knocking him backwards off his chair, Hoghorn was blown physically across the table, throwing her Victorian starched pleats over her head, revealing a red basque, matching stockings and suspenders, complete with a vivid purple garter around her thigh. The Major and Waller-Boyce had instinctively ducked and escaped the full force of the explosion and marvelled at the scene now presented before them. Both their eyes landed on Hoghorn in her mistress attire. For a woman her age, she had an exceptional body. She raised herself up, smoothing her dress back down, hoping nobody had noticed.

Waller-Boyce's attention was drawn to Smallpott, who was flat on his back and struggling to get up. He grasped his wrist and pulled him upright, at the same time sliding back Smallpott's jacket and shirt sleeve, revealing several crude hand-made tattoos favoured by the lower ranks. Neither said anything. It was then, that Waller-Boyce saw Smallpott had the army pistol in his other hand, as did the Major who leaped heroically towards Smallpott, bringing him crashing to the ground for a second time. He wrested the weapon out of his grasp and put it in his pocket. None of this was seen by the others, who where generally choking in the fine mist of talcum powder.

'Let him go,' said Waller-Boyce 'He'll be no trouble anymore, I'm sure.' With that, Smallpott scurried away like a rat leaving a sinking ship. 'Fresh air I think, don't you?' finished Waller-Boyce.

Fortunately, the blast area had been minimal and other than a bright flash and a fine coating of powder, no serious damage was done. Hoghorn and Smallpott might not have agreed.

That evening, a party was held in the village square that rivalled Burnt Cow Day itself. Everyone attended, with the notable exception of Reginald Smallpott and Chastity Hoghorn. They had driven off together earlier, with their cases packed. As they passed the inn and the three new Lords of the manor sat outside in the evening sun, Smallpott smiled. Hoghorn, however, remained aloof. 'He took that well,' said the Major.

'Not surprisingly, considering he's got a boot full your small Renoir's and Monet's.' answered Waller-Boyce

The Majors mouth opened but nothing left it.

'Not to worry, he only thinks he has.

'How. . . when?' eventually escaped the Major.

'Years ago, he'd been taking the smaller pictures to London to be cleaned and valued, a suggestion I think he may have implanted with your mother. He also had them expertly copied and it was these he re-hung in the hall. They must have cost a small fortune at the time, especially having to have the backs copied as well in case they were rearranged or casually inspected.

'And the originals?' murmured the Major.

'Stored in an ice-box attached to the side of Riverside Cottage, a legacy from its past fishing use, I suspect. I think he was hedging his bets, he knew he might get a cash bequest through his, shall we say 'friendship' with your mother but his real investment were the paintings themselves, so you can imagine his delight when on your mothers death, he learnt he might inherit the whole shebang anyway.'

'So he put them back?'

'Had to - and quickly, old Makepeace would be doing an inventory and although I'm sure he wasn't an art expert but if he did spot something amiss, Smallpott would be in the frame, to coin a suitable phrase. Especially as the cleaning receipts, with his name on, would have gone on the household accounts.' finished Waller-Boyce.

'So now', started the Major slowly, 'you say he's got a boot full of fakes but he thinks they're genuine, so at some point very recently, he swapped them back, yes?'

'Yes and no, I swapped them back beforehand and so when he swapped them, he was actually replacing the fakes with the real ones, they were that good - and it wasn't him, it was her, Hoghorn.

'Hoghorn, devious bitch. Sorry, I forgot she was your mother.' reined in the Major.

'It's alright, there's no love lost there, I can assure you.'

'What sort of hold did Smallpott have over her then, were they lovers?' queried the major.'

'Now this is the great unanswered question that has been bothering me for some time. I dismissed the idea of a physical relationship until that rather revealing glimpse during Makepeace's rather explosive finale.'

'A sight now engraved on my mind.' added the Major.

'Yes, indeed' continued Waller-Boyce-Stonely, 'I still don't think there was that sort of connection, I'm rather inclined to think her apparel was a homage to your . . . our father. It is possible that their relationship was a discrete but lengthy sexual one, favouring a Mistress and slave arrangement.'

The Majors mind drew a vision of his naked father shackled, whipped and begging for more 'correction' in some dark corner of the cellar. It would account for the 'leather sundries' mentioned in his fathers diary.

'Did you notice the locket around her neck?'

'I had a feeling she had one, how did you find out?' asked the Major in sheer wonder at his half brothers deductive powers.

'When she fainted in the inn, Shirley undid a couple of her top buttons and I caught a brief glimpse of a heart-shaped clasp. As someone who rarely, if ever, ventured out of the village, it had to contain something very dear indeed, perhaps a lock of our fathers hair, or mine when I was born.'

'All well and good but it doesn't answer what hold Smallpott had over her.' queried the Major.

'No it doesn't, I'm afraid, I can but guess that some sort of agreement was reached between them. Hoghorn is an intelligent woman and would have seen through Smallpott in an instant and after the death of the Duke she found herself with nothing other than domestic service to look forward to, a grace and favour home until she could no longer work and a small pension, I should imagine. I wouldn't be at all surprised if it was Hoghorn herself, who steered Smallpott to the grander prize of fine art, she knew their value and had unquestioned access. So by helping Smallpott, she would have a very agreeable retirement.

'How did you manage get into the house unnoticed?'

Waller-Boyce smiled at his new half brother.

'Hardly a challenge really, you and Henderson always had a cigarette together in the boathouse in the evenings, Hoghorn was my only concern but by eight she was gone, I just walked in plain and simple. In fact I spent two nights in the music room under the dust sheets, very comfortable I can tell you.'

The Major smiled. 'It looks like we're going to have to get another house-keeper and cook then.' said the Major, with more than a little relief.

'Indeed, but the cook can wait, I much prefer the Inns dining arrangements.' answered Waller-Boyce-Stonely.

'Here, here, added the Major, 'an arrangement young Timothy I'm sure, would agree to.'

'I forgot to thank you for throwing yourself at Smallpott when you spotted the gun.'

'It was nothing, you're family after all.'

Waller-Boyce smiled as he played with the bullets in his jacket pocket.

'What are your plans now?' asked the Major as the two of them walked up the gravel drive to the Hall after the festivities had drawn to a natural close.

'How do you mean?'

'You know my involvement in the black-market business in India, you've got enough to put me away for a long time, finally clear your desk as it were, one last success.

'Yes, this is true, and what will the Army do I wonder, deal with it the same way they dealt with all my cases, hide it away because it's an embarrassment to them. They don't like exposing their weaknesses. There were no medals for uncovering mistakes in that business, no promotion either. There was a hint of bitterness in his voice.

Waller-Boyce stopped and took the lighter out of his pocket and re-lit his pipe. The polished brass, underneath the worn silver plating, caught the glow of the full moon for a moment. 'For 34 years service' was still just legible but his name had long since gone. He looked up at the Hall before him and the surrounding land and trees, a bird spotter's paradise in a quiet oasis. There was a dull metallic clink as the lighter hit the drain cover and came to rest, teetering on the edge of the grill. Waller-Boyce nudged it down the dark slot with the toe of his shoe.

'You must teach me how the distillery works, Rupert,' he said, as he caught up with the Major and put his hand on his shoulder.

'How did you know?'

'There aren't many villages with alcohol dripping from a statues cock.'

Timothy had taken the battered Morris Eight back to Customs House on Monday and resigned. He collected his mug and made arrangements for his little bungalow to be sold, before returning to his new home in the countryside. He stopped off at the Stonely Arms for a pint.

'Ah, here comes my Italian friend.' said Shirley, as he entered the bar.

'I don't get it.' said Timothy, until Shirley cupped the front of his trousers firmly.

'Oh.'

'Home for good now, are we?' she smiled.
'Oh, yes.'
'So I'm in for a good rogering later on?'
'Oh, yes.'

Mr Reginald Burrows and his dominant, straight-laced older sister, opened a small bed and breakfast house in Cornwall. It had some nice pictures on the wall. Business was adequate.

About the author

James Henry was born in Surrey, England. He moved down to the south coast at an early age to be with his mother. (He had to, he was a baby). James received a normal, secondary education but was blessed with also being able to read and write. He pursued a career of nothing in particular but enjoyed writing until his pen ran out. Later life brought an interest in doing something that would really move people - he became a bus driver. He bought another pen.

James's first book 'Driver, do you stop at the station?' was a humorous look behind the scenes of becoming a bus driver and proved to be quite popular.

An English Custom, is James's first 'proper book', as he calls it. A novel collection of words, joined together with other words, forming sentences which later became paragraphs. "It's a proper story with a beginning, middle and end, I'm so proud."

James Henry is married to his wife and has children.

Acknowledgments:
Lloyd Bayley – The most English Australian I know

17097631R00080

Printed in Great Britain
by Amazon